A DIET

IS THE

LAST THING

YOU NEED

WEIGHT LOSS
&
MAINTENANCE
ANSWERS

Brenda L. Wolfe, Ph.D.

ISBN   978-0-578-95016-7 (ePub)
       978-0-578-95017-4 (Print)
       978-0-578-32012-0 (Kindle ebook)

APPRECIATION
&
DEDICATION

Over the decades I have had the privilege of learning from brilliant clinicians, clinical scientists, and community mental health experts. At McGill University, University of California, and University of New Mexico I have enjoyed the intellectual acrobatics of melding scientific inquiry with community wisdom, and learned to develop evidence-based programs that make sense to the people they are intended to serve. To my teachers, mentors, and role models, thank you.

I also wish to thank my patients. Over the years I have worked with thousands of individuals struggling to make sense of the vagaries of life and, in particular, to make peace with their bodies. It is from these men and women that I learned how to translate the 'right' way to do things into the 'realistic' way. In helping them, I became better able to help others. It is to these brave, hard-working individuals that I dedicate this book.

CONTENTS

PREFACE

This book will never sell a million copies.
I will never be a millionaire.

If I wanted to be a millionaire, I would promise you the secret to weight loss by chocolate or fine wine, or both. Since I will not tell you the chocolate secret, I clearly do not want to be a millionaire. Instead, I am going to tell you how your excess weight is the result of you having grievously mistimed your birth—by about 10,000 years! I am also going to give you the questions and answers that will help you work around that bit of bad timing and live at a more comfortable weight.

My goal is to help you gain an accurate and deeper understanding of the forces that feed overweight and obesity so that you can make intelligent decisions about how to manage your weight. We have no shortage of diet doctors and celebrity know-it-alls waiting to sell you programs or products—some of which may be somewhat helpful. Most, however, will at best help for a short period of time until you tire of them, revert to your natural lifestyle, and give up and regain.

As a clinical psychologist specializing in the treatment of obesity and eating disorders, I have helped thousands of people figure out how best to approach their weight management challenges. While there is no one-size-fits-all solution, I have learned from research and experience that there are better and worse ways to approach the design of individual solutions. Over the course of this book, I will guide you in determining what goals are realistic *for you*. I will teach you how to outsmart your personal landmines and revise your internal dialogue to make the change that gently shapes your lifestyle to achieve your weight and health goals.

By the time you have worked your way through this book, you will likely no longer feel the need for a formal diet program. However, if you do, having made the changes herein, you will find it easier to select a program that works well for you and easier to work that program effectively. In other words, while I doubt you will need a diet, I know for sure that a diet is the last thing you (may) need.

CHAPTER 1

IMPORTANT THINGS TO KNOW

Before you start, you need to know *and accept* something. That is, you will never look like your favorite movie star. Nor will you have the body of your sexiest friend, or your personal trainer. The only body you can achieve with any weight management strategy is a healthier version of yourself—which results from the interplay between your genes, your environment, and your actions. In other words, you *can* achieve a lifelong healthier weight if you set your sights on shaping your environment and actions to *work with* your genetic givens. Fighting your genes is an unwinnable battle; save your energy for something fun.

The first important thing successful weight-managers learn is that weight is a reflection of how genetics and lifestyle interact. If you come from a long line of tall thin people and earn your living digging ditches and carrying bricks, you almost assuredly are not overweight. If you come from a family that tends to be heavier and you spend your days staring at a screen, skinny is unlikely in the cards for you without focus and a whole lot of obsessive energy. So, any program or product described as "fast," "guaranteed," "easy," "effortless," or any other awesome adjective, may be exciting but will not be effective for long.

Changing your weight comes from changing the way you go

through life. It requires *realistic planning* and *daily attention*. Of course, a good sales pitch can convince you that you are ready to radically change your life right now, but if that were possible, would you be reading this book? Of course not—you would not need it. You tried those programs, bought those books, and are still struggling. *Realistic planning* begins with deciding to make small meaningful changes at a pace that minimizes discomfort. *Daily attention* means that even when you are engaged in activities that have no obvious link to weight management, they are embedded within the larger context of 'lifestyle' that does indeed affect your weight. If this sounds abstract, consider the scenario in which you are reading a good book in your favorite chair. While that has nothing *obvious* to do with weight, flesh out the scenario with a bowl of chocolates on your lap … Not so abstract now, is it?

At the risk of sounding like I *am* pitching a sale, I will now tell you that the changes you need to make are "simple." Nothing in this approach is complicated because the only effective way to modify your weight over the long run is to make small changes that fit your life and do so at a reasonable pace. There is no need to learn new jargon or get in touch with your inner child (or parent or inner Jedi). So, no complicated changes. However, changing lifelong patterns is not easy. It requires effort. The amount of effort varies depending on your mood and particular focus at the moment. It is not necessarily an exhausting venture but definitely one that requires effort. Hence, *simple but not easy*.

Another truth you must accept is that *there is no perfect*. Neither humans nor our efforts can be perfect; we can be awfully good, occasionally brilliant, but never perfect. I mention this because the goal to do something perfectly is frequently a cause of failure. In fact, as the 18th Century writer/philosopher Voltaire said (in

French so forgive the imperfect translation), "Perfect is the enemy of good." Striving for perfection interferes with success in two ways. One is that since perfection is impossible, you ultimately end up wasting valuable resources spinning wheels that take you nowhere. The other way perfection causes trouble is when it is part of your definition of success. If your plan is to do everything I tell you to do, all the time exactly as I describe it, you are going to fail miserably. First off, you cannot do anything perfectly. Second, if your goal is to be perfect and you are imperfect, you instantly fail just by setting the goal, and then risk losing your drive and giving up altogether. (More about this in Chapter 3.)

In place of aiming to be perfect, or even super-awesome, I recommend you aim for 'good enough.' Read everything in this book, think about it, and implement most of it as consistently as you can at the time. It will be more effective if you keep doing whatever you can, than if you try to do everything perfectly and consequently burn out. Some of the changes will be easy for you, others not—treat yourself as you would a youngster you are teaching to read. You would not expect the child to read Voltaire (even in English) right after introducing the alphabet. You would not expect the child to recognize all 26 letters of the alphabet right away. You would praise recognition of the first few letters, celebrate a few more, and so on until the little cutie was reading Voltaire and Shakespeare. Allow yourself the same leeway to work hard at your own pace. That is good enough to get you where you want to go.

If I have not scared you off with talk of simple but hard and no chance of perfection, that means you are ready to give up roller-coaster diets and impossible exercise regimens. It means you are not afraid to make yourself a little uncomfortable in the moment in order to improve the overall long-term comfort of living in your body. It means you have finally figured out that if it takes you longer to reach your desired weight than is promised by television doctors, that is a worthwhile trade-off not to have to lose the same dang pounds over and over again. If all that is true, this book is for you.

Most self-help books, especially those about weight loss, include a section toward the end about 'maintenance.' This book does not for the simple reason that if you do not start 'maintaining' right now, there will be nothing to maintain at the end. Let me explain.

Having decided to make time to read this book, you must maintain that decision; maintain the effort to keep reading and maintain the focus to retain what you read. The first step you take toward change must be maintained so you can build upon it with the next step. Each time you make a little change, you must maintain that change in order for it to have an impact. In other words, if you do not think about maintenance before you hit your final weight target, chances are slim that you will hit your target; it is more likely you will wander off the path. Hence, rather than power through a diet as you have undoubtedly done many times in the past, this time you will make small changes to your lifestyle, each of which you will maintain, so that as your weight approaches your desired range, what you have been doing to get there has simply become how you live. Moreover, along the way you will have waffled in how consistently you have 'maintained,' often having to stop and figure out what went wrong, correct yourself, and reset. (In other words, nothing perfect about it.) You will have to maintain attention to your behavior but as time goes on, the behavior will feel increasingly natural and require less effort.

When I work with patients one-on-one, the questions and challenges they bring to our sessions drive the order and fashion in which I share with them the decades of obesity science on which I base my guidance. Obviously, that sort of individualized sequencing cannot happen between you, the reader, and me. Hence, in the spirit of simplicity, I have organized almost everything you need to know to achieve a more comfortable weight into 10 chapters that roughly reflect the most common order in which I work with in-person patients. Chapter 1, which you are currently reading, addresses realistic expectations for the journey you are undertaking, orients you to the life domains (topics) we will address, and explains the structure of the approach.

Chapter 2—Blueprint, outlines 10 core behaviors that everyone must incorporate in order to achieve consistent and satisfying weight management. However, while these behaviors are necessary, they are not sufficient. I have included this chapter to accommodate readers who are impatient to start NOW. Those readers can begin on these 10 actions now and continue reading so they understand the why and how of them, as well as learn how to change their thinking to make the actions easier to implement. If you are patient and plan to read the entire book, feel free to skip Chapter 2.

Chapter 3—Foundation, addresses those issues that are important to consider before starting to make changes to your life. I can tell you with 100% certainty that failure to take these things into account is one of the most common reasons that diet books and programs sell so well—people don't lay a solid foundation and end up jumping from one failed plan or book to the next. It is great for the diet business—not so great for the dieter. *Foundation* begins with an overview of the reasons so many humans are overweight (that relates to the 10,000-year issue mentioned earlier) and walks you through figuring out the best way for *you* to approach weight management.

With the groundwork firmly laid, we move on to *Chapter 4* which focuses on the thing most people ignore until they lose it—*Motivation*. This could reasonably have been included with *Foundation* but is so critically important that it merits its very own chapter. Taking time now to understand and capture your enthusiasm about getting a handle on your habits will save you frustration, disappointment, and the price of more self-help books down the road.

The effect of the environment on people's food choices, and consequently on their weight, has been well documented in psychology and food-marketing labs for decades. From the moment we are born, internal sensations such as hunger and satiety and fatigue and happiness have been linked with external food events so often and in so many ways that it is often difficult to know whether we are hungry or simply looking at an especially luscious chunk of chocolate. The answers in *Chapter 5—Environment & Hunger,* will help you wrest more control of your food choices from the outside world.

Chapter 6 explores *Food & Hunger* which often travel together but not always. This chapter answers basic questions like "What is Food?" and complicated questions about the best foods and eating schedules for you, and how to recognize when you have had enough to eat. One would think that in today's world where the knowledge of a thousand experts is mere keystrokes away, it would be rare to meet anyone who did not understand the basics about food. Yet, in my practice I meet those people every day—they are not rare! Almost all could cite chapter and verse of every diet plan under the sun, yet few understand how to select foods that nourish *and* please *and* help them achieve healthier weights.

Chapter 7—Emotions & Hunger, gives you a better understanding of how your emotions feed hunger and how food and eating affect your emotions. You will also learn to tell the difference between them. They often feel so much alike that you find yourself seeking snacks when what you really need is a hug or seeking hugs when what you really need is a sandwich.

Chapter 8 addresses *Exercise*—it is easier than you think. I will leave you with that teaser.

Beginning with Chapter 3, the information is presented as a series of questions and answers to keep it straight forward and easy to read. Chapters 3 through 8 each conclude with a section called *Roundup* that summarizes the key ideas and specific steps outlined in the chapter.

Beginning with Chapter 4, each *Roundup* section is followed by a segment called *Maintenance Minder* designed to help you recognize and build on your forward movement.

Following the *Maintenance Minder* in each of Chapters 3 through 8, are segments titled *For Parents*. If you and/or your child's other parent are overweight or obese, there is a good likelihood your child will follow suit. This is not due to the child's inheritance of your DNA, nor to the environment in which you are raising the child, nor to how you model food choice and activity. ***It is due to a combination of all three factors.*** The younger your child when you begin your own shift to a healthier lifestyle, the easier it will be for him or her to avoid having to face the weight challenges that plague you. Except under extreme circumstances, medical providers rarely recommend that children be put on diets. Moreover, except under extremely extreme (!) circumstances, mental health experts strongly **recommend that children are not ever put on diets.** What is recommended, is that parents structure the home and the family's activities to promote healthy intake and healthy activity, facilitating appropriate food intake that allows the child to grow into his or her weight, rather than trying to force weight loss through caloric restriction. Each *For Parents* segment will outline how to apply the material from that chapter to promote positive growth for your child.

Chapter 9—Miscellaneous, contains additional questions that do not neatly fit into the preceding chapters but nonetheless are relevant to my goal of providing you a comprehensive understanding of the forces that drive your weight challenges and the strategies that may be helpful in defining your own solution. Also included in this chapter is critical guidance on how to evaluate the 'proof' boasted by advertisements promising to change your life.

Finally, *Chapter 10—Next Steps* helps you organize your thinking as you move ahead. Along with reviewing the key decisions you have made as you worked through this book, it helps you plan future goals. Most importantly, this chapter sets the stage for you to begin taking on the role of being your own therapist as it answers the question, "What questions should I ask myself?" In the unlikely event that at this point you have implemented most of my recommendations fairly consistently but have not begun to lose weight, you will learn what to do to change that.

I encourage you *not* to read the entire book in one sitting. There are two reasons for this. One is that information is better retained if you take breaks while absorbing it rather than muscle through everything in one long session. The other reason is that most of the answers point to something you can do to help yourself. In some cases, it is a different way to think about your body and your goals, in others it is a change you can make to your environment or your action patterns. Taking the time to think about and incorporate the information will increase your ability to make the changes permanent, and hence make your healthy weight your lifelong weight.

Along with answers to the questions, scattered throughout you will find *Action Items* and *Stories.* The *Action Items* point you to something specific you need to think about or do. The *Stories* from my clinical work (protecting everyone's identity of course) will make the information a little clearer, a little more fun, and a little easier to use.

So, sit down, put your feet up, and let's get started.

CHAPTER 2

BLUEPRINT

As you have figured out, I am not going to give you a detailed set of instructions designed to result in quick weight loss if you follow them perfectly. What I am providing is a set of guidelines to help reshape your behavior so that your relationship with food and exercise becomes one that lends itself to more easily making choices that allow you to live more comfortably.

For your efforts to have significant and lasting effects, you will need to move more slowly than you have with diets in the past. Take your time to think about the concepts I share with you and invest energy in implementing the strategies I outline. Count today as Day 1 of your journey toward a healthier weight, *and then stop counting—because the journey is the destination*. Thinking about the choices you make and making small changes to how you think and what you do will create a lifestyle that results in a healthier weight and healthier body. My hope is that you mindfully read all the answers in this book, even those that may not seem relevant to you at the moment, and allow the information to color your approach to day-to-day decisions. Even though the material speaks explicitly about weight management, much of it is equally applicable to management of anxiety, depression, and interpersonal challenges. Hence, answers that do not speak directly to your immediate weight-related problem, may inadvertently help with a different problem. As you know, everything in life ultimately is interrelated.

No two of the thousands of patients with whom I have worked struggled in exactly the same way or progressed at exactly the same rate. However, regardless of the nuances of their individual needs, there is a core set of behaviors that everyone needed to learn and adopt. Although these behaviors by themselves are not sufficient to take you where you want to go, they are the minimally necessary steps you must take to make lifelong weight management a reality. You can think of them as a blueprint—a line drawing to get you started on a beautifully constructed life. The why's and how's of implementing them are found in the chapters that follow.

1. Set a realistic target weight range. Consider your genetics, your lifestyle, and your preferences before you decide on what you 'should' weigh.
2. Commit to daily tracking of food intake, as well as food- and exercise-related behavior.
3. Begin a weight graph which you update once each week on a consistent pre-specified day.
4. Think deeply about both the pros and the cons of losing weight, as well as of not losing weight.
5. Review your weight and dieting history to identify and plan for situations that repeatedly interfere with your intended behaviors and set you up for weight regain.
6. Adopt a Designated Eating Place at home and at work or school. Make this the only place you eat.
7. Do not engage in activities other than conversation or listening to music while you are eating.

8. Whenever you have food in your mouth, make sure your hands are empty. Do not hold food or utensils or begin preparing the next bite while you are still chewing or swallowing.
9. Slowly increase the amount of physical activity you do each day.
10. Each day, eat three meals and two or three snacks comprised of carbohydrates, fat, and protein, while keeping your total caloric intake below your current level.

CHAPTER 3

FOUNDATION

To build a good house, one must lay a sound foundation—one that is level and strong so the house neither tilts nor topples. The same applies to managing your weight. The strong, level foundation of weight management is understanding the forces that shape human body weight and your idiosyncratic way of responding to those forces. This chapter will help you lay a foundation for lifelong weight management.

The questions in this chapter are grouped into those analogous to preparing the ground for your foundation, pouring the cement, and hardening it.

PREPARING THE GROUND

Ensuring your safety and understanding the forces that shape weight-related behavior are essential first steps in enhancing your ability to manage your weight.

Do I have an eating disorder?

Overweight and obesity are not Eating Disorders (EDs). While obesity is considered a medical disorder, weighing more than is healthy or desirable is not an ED. However, EDs do sometimes result in excess weight and EDs do not usually go away on their own; hence, the need to address this question.

The table below describes behaviors and feelings associated with EDs. If any of them apply to you, please consult a psychotherapist who specializes in the treatment of EDs before you attempt to change your weight. It is common for people with EDs to believe that if they could get their weight where they want it, everything else would get better too. Sadly, they are dead wrong (and it sometimes kills them dead). Happily, if you do have an ED, there is effective treatment that can help you find peace.

You may have an eating disorder if any of the following are true for you:
• You have episodes of eating during which you feel out of control and eat amounts of food that leave you feeling ashamed of yourself and/or uncomfortably full.
• You attempt to 'undo' food intake you think was excessive by making yourself vomit, using laxatives or other drugs, and/or doing a lot of extra exercise.
• The size or shape of your body is so important to you that concerns about it often interfere with your ability to enjoy the people and activities of your life.
• Whether or not you like yourself depends to a very great extent on your weight.
• Your family and friends tell you that you are too thin but mostly what you see when you look at yourself is fat.
• You find it difficult to eat on days that you feel bigger or do not like the number on the scale.

NOTE: Good online sources of information and help finding a therapist are: National Eating Disorders Association (https://www.nationaleatingdisorders.org/) and Academy of Eating Disorders (https://www.aedweb.org).

Must I see a doctor before I start?

Most of the recommended changes in this book do not need medical clearance. If you truly follow my lead and *gently* shift your behavior to change how you think about body, food, and exercise, and minimize mindless eating, you should be able to safely move forward. However, if you have (or suspect you have) a physical condition that requires a specific dietary or exercise regimen, definitely consult with your physician before making changes. Also, if you have experienced a recent dramatic change in your weight (up or down) for which you do not know the reason, see your physician.

Finally, if you are overweight and no weight loss occurs as you lessen your food intake and increase your physical activity, this may be a sign of a metabolic condition (e.g., hypothyroid, insulin resistance). Your physician can diagnose and treat these problems. In most cases, with treatment, weight management becomes easier.

Is there a shortcut?

No. Getting from here to the healthier weight you want requires your attention—pretty much every day from today until you decide you no longer care about your health. So if you are after quick and easy, donate this book to your local library and either throw your money in the trash or give it to a (charlatan) product or program that promises to do the work for you. On the other hand, if you are after lifelong weight management, keep reading and you can get there.

How do I control my weight?

You cannot. No one can. We can control actions that influence our weight, but we cannot control our weight. Body weight is the result of the effect of your actions and environment on your biology, and the effect of your biology on your actions. You can, to varying degrees, control your actions and your environment. You can even influence your biology (e.g., choosing to watch a scary movie can make your heart race). However, you cannot impose your will on your weight. If you could, I am fairly sure that you already would have chosen to be your optimal weight and you would not have needed this book.

How often should I weigh myself?

In my experience, it is most useful to weigh yourself once each week on the same day at the same time in the morning, before you have eaten, and wearing the same clothing (or no clothing at all). Weighing more often is likely to drive you crazy as you react to the normal day-to-day variations of the living organism you are. Weighing less often may make it too easy to put off for tomorrow actions best taken today.

Should I graph my weight?

Yes! A visual representation of your progress will both be motivating and help you stay calm when there is either no decrease or an uptick. It is 100% normal and expected that your weight will not follow a smooth downward line. Progress is measured in terms of a downward *trend*, even when there may be weeks that the line does not go down, or goes up a bit. This is a natural part of the process; if you remain focused on the changes you make over the course of this book, your weight will trend downward.

It is helpful to mark the upper and lower lines of your target weight range (see *Hardening the Cement* later in this chapter) on the graph to illustrate progress toward your goal. Below is an example of how this might look. Notice that there were many weeks that this person's weight did not decrease, and several when it increased. Taking it all in stride and giving more attention to behaviors than to the number on the scale ultimately resulted in sufficient weight loss to achieve the target range which is indicated by the two heavy horizontal lines.

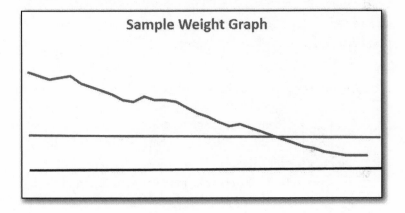

Why should I have lived 10,000 years ago?

The world for which we are built is one of long distances traveled on foot. As a species, we are healthiest when we walk many miles a day looking for edible plants and break a sweat tracking and hunting meat. In other words, our bodies are beautifully built to survive a hard-to-get food supply. That is our native environment.

We have the extraordinary ability to remain focused on the food search despite growing hunger, and to efficiently store energy (in the form of fat) to keep us alive when our search is not successful. Also part of this beautiful design is our drive to eat whenever and as long as food is available to ensure we have reserves on board for times of scarcity. So, up until about 10,000 years ago we spent tremendous amounts of energy getting food, and ate as much as we could when we found it to ensure sufficient stored energy (fat) to survive famines. It was a time during which Weight Watchers would have been bankrupt in its first week!

Had you the good sense to have lived at that time, you would not be reading this book because there would have been no market for books such as this one. You would have almost no likelihood of being obese and if you were overweight, your family and friends would be envious of your excellent ability to survive food shortages.

Action Item

Think about daily living differences between your 21st Century life and the one you would have lived 10,000 years ago. Here is a hint:

- No wheels—feet were your mode of transportation.
- No motors—speed required you to move!
- Obtaining food required walking and sweating.
- No refrigerators to allow stocking up to avoid another food chase tomorrow or next week.
- Food could be eaten raw or cooked over fire, but not microwaved in two minutes or tenderized in the slow-cooker while you watch a movie (also no movies).
- No electric mixers, bread machines, automatic coffee-makers.
- Talking to someone not within yelling distance required walking.

Just for fun, estimate how many hours during an average week you would be on your feet if you had to live like your 10,000-year-old cousin. Consider how long it would take you to walk to work or school, what effort would be required to bring food home, how much time might be spent preparing food from scratch ...

Now do two things. First *forgive yourself for the weight struggle*. It is not your fault. It is no one's fault. (Unless you want to blame your parents for having you so late on the cosmic timeline. But that is between you and them; none of my business.) Then, **decide to add a few steps to most of the routine things you do each day**. For instance, park a row further from your destination, walk the entire length of the mall each way before you begin shopping, when you take your dog out to do its 'business,' make it a real walk and not a quick poop'n'scoop.

We will address physical activity in greater detail in the Exercise chapter. For now, commit to finding opportunities to move a little more.

Given my birthdate, what's my option?

Given that your body is built for a native environment you cannot possibly inhabit, you have two options. One is to spend your life frustrated and annoyed as you go from diet to diet, losing and gaining weight. The other option is that you figure out what weight range is achievable given your lifestyle, genetics, and interests.

Juan

Juan was in his mid-30s when he sought help for his seriously expanding waistline. He had been a high-school athlete and remained physically active throughout college.

Since graduating, however, he found it difficult to make time for group sports and hated the gym. With a desk job and a growing family, Juan figured his only option was to diet. He set his sights on his weight at college graduation and searched the internet to find a plan that would get him to that weight most quickly. And he did great on it! His family was super-supportive and he was able to get through multiple social events, including December holidays parties, without slipping up. Juan lost all the weight he targeted— and gained it all back, plus some. He did this about three times before he came to my office.

You will hear more about Juan later. For now, the important thing to know is he ultimately did achieve long-term weight management but in a totally different way than he expected. The first thing he did was lose the ridiculous notion that at age 38 with a sedentary job, two kids, and a spouse who performed miracles in the kitchen, he could have the physique of a 22-year-old athlete. He revised his goal taking into account his current lifestyle and preferences.

Should I just eat naturally?

If I had a nickel for every patient who told me that they wanted to learn to eat "naturally," meaning only eat when and as long as hungry, I would be drowning in nickels! What I teach my patients, is that eating "naturally" means eating as much of whatever foods we can find, when we find them. In our natural environment (which we will call our "native" environment from here on), that ensured we ate our fill when food was available, which it often was not. Hence, excess weight was seldom a problem. The other aspect of our native environment that prevented our natural eating habits from making us obese is that the food was not as calorically dense as is our modern processed food supply.

Today the problem is that unless you are impoverished, food is consistently accessible, calorically dense, and getting it requires minimal energy expenditure. Unlike was the case in our pre-historic home, eating naturally in our current environment is usually eating too much.

NOTE: And if you are indeed impoverished, for heaven's sake, buy food instead of books about eating!

Can I just listen to my body?

For most people, bodily hunger and satiety signals tend to be fairly subtle—for good reason. Think again about our native environment. If at the very moment our energy reserves began to drop we were bombarded with roaring hunger signals, it would be difficult to concentrate on the task of finding food. We would be far too distracted to hunt or gather effectively. Hunger signals start softly and increase in volume as our fuel reserves drop. In this way, we do not forget to eat but can concentrate well enough to find food.

NOTE: It is also noteworthy that when fuel levels drop dangerously low, hunger signals again lose volume. This is, in part, what happens with the eating disorder Anorexia Nervosa when the individual excessively restricts food intake. After a while, the ability to recognize the need for food is lost. Untreated, this ultimately results in death.

Satiety signals tend to be even weaker than hunger signals. This too makes sense if you consider our native environment. Perhaps we find a ripe non-poisonous berry bush today or perhaps not.

Maybe the animal we have been tracking will be dinner tonight or maybe not. (Or maybe we will be dinner … but that is another story.) After so many miles and so much effort, which translates into so many calories burned, it would be suicide to take only a "reasonable" serving of food. After all, who knew what tomorrow would bring in terms of food-finding success! Given that uncertainty, those of our ancestors who survived to produce us tended to have easily ignored satiety signals and the capacity to eat well beyond what was needed for that day's activities.

What is signal deafness?

Adding insult to injury if you are an experienced dieter, you so thoroughly have practiced ignoring hunger and satiety signals that even if your body began life with a strong 'voice,' so to speak, you have become quite good at ignoring it. In other words, you have deafened yourself to your body's signals.

Figuring out how your body lets you know when it needs food and when it has received enough food for the time being, will be key to improving your eating habits. Without enhancing your ability to 'hear' your body, you will be forever stuck trying to adhere to an eating regimen that may meet your nutritional needs, but almost assuredly will not meet your enjoyment needs.

The process of learning to recognize your internal signals is a meandering one. With the *Stomach Exercise* (see next question), you will begin to identify the changes that occur in your body as your fuel levels drop and then increase with food intake. Over time, though, both the signals and your ability to perceive them may change which is why I say this is a meandering process.

What is the Stomach Exercise?

The Stomach Exercise is designed to help you recognize the unique signals your body sends when your stomach is empty and your blood sugar levels (i.e., available fuel) are running low. To effectively accomplish this, you must make sure your stomach truly is empty before starting the exercise. In addition, you should repeat the exercise at least three times on three different days as body sensations do fluctuate with changing circumstances; your objective is to **capture the general sense** of how your body lets you know when it needs to be fed and when it is no longer hungry. Here is how to do it.

PREPARATION

Schedule the exercise for a day on which you can prepare a full meal for the time you usually have your largest meal. Also, make sure you can eat without too many distractions so do not plan this for a meal that includes guests. Other than adequately hydrating, do not eat anything for three or four hours before the Stomach Exercise to ensure your belly is indeed empty. This way, you know for sure that you are physically hungry. Ahead of time, prepare a full-sized sheet of paper with the diagram shown here. The empty oval represents your empty stomach and the arrows marked *Inventory* point to empty, ½-way, ¾-way, and full levels.

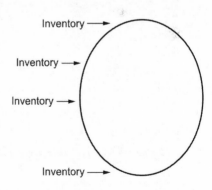

WARNING

If you have a medical condition that requires you be relatively precise about when and what you eat, do not disrupt that schedule for this exercise. Simply avoid *unnecessary* food intake during the hours preceding each time you do the exercise.

INSTRUCTIONS

Seated at the table in front of your meal with your prepared diagram beside your plate, imagine the oval to be your empty stomach. Before you begin eating, take a mental inventory of your body from head to toe and next to the bottom of the empty oval record the *physical sensations* you notice in each body part. Mentally scan for *physical* sensations in your feet and legs, hands and arms, belly, chest, and head. Record your observations on the diagram next to the bottom of the oval. These physical sensations (e.g., temperature, muscle tension, cramping, gurgling, aching, etc.) are your body's hunger signals. It is unlikely you will notice sensations in all areas; record only those you do.

Then begin eating mindfully by following the *Mouth/Hand Rule* (i.e., nothing in your hands while there is food in your mouth). After every three or four mouthfuls, stop and draw a line across the oval to indicate how full you imagine your stomach to be at that point. When your lines reach ½, ¾, and the top of the oval, stop and record another body inventory.

Repeat this exercise on at least three different days. While it is likely that some of the signals you notice will prove to be standard for your body, others may either not be consistently recurrent or not appear the first time you do this but appear during later efforts. In fact, you may find that you have a variety of signals, not all of which show up each time. The key is to get into the habit of paying attention to your body.

INTERPRETATION

When you review your notes, look for repeated patterns across the three (or more) meals. Using myself as an example, the three consistent signals I get when hunger builds are stomach rumbles and grumbles (a tad embarrassing depending on circumstances!), slight tension in my upper body, and cold hands. As I begin eating, my stomach quiets, my muscles relax, and my hands warm up. There is no noticeable signal associated with my full belly other than disappearance of hunger signals, and the food does not have the same compelling attraction it had when I was hungry. Your body will have its own set of recognizable signals.

As you consider your results, also pay attention to how much food you actually ate by the time the lines you drew approached the top of the oval/stomach. Almost every single person who has done this exercise has been surprised to discover how much less food she or he needs to be 'full' than previously thought. You can use this knowledge to retrain your brain to link more moderate amounts of food with fullness and satisfaction.

Action Item

Despite how odd this exercise may appear, and I assure you more than a few patients were skeptical, ***The Stomach Exercise*** is powerful. You will be astounded at how subtle but discernable are the changes in your body as you eat. Moreover, your bodily signals of hunger and satiety are unique to you so there is no shortcut to be found on

Wikipedia or Google. Decide now which three days this week you are going to do it. Then do it!

Behavior Logs? (Ugh)

If you have ever kept a food diary for more than five minutes, you know that the simple act of recording your intake almost always results in eating less. In fact, one of the most reliable predictors of successful weight management is the keeping of food records. Whether you record your intake in a paper notebook, a computer spreadsheet, a smart phone application, or a pile of sticky notes, recording it moves eating out of the mindless see-it-eat-it realm of our ancestors, and into your mindful control.

Recording your intake makes you aware. Recording before eating (ideal) or immediately after (good) or later in the day (better than no records), forces you to actively think about what you are eating. That in itself often stimulates you to adjust your portion size or make a healthier choice.

Camila

My favorite story about the power of Behavior Logs is that of Camila. She was a single mother of two children under age 10. Juggling a demanding job with daycare drop-off and pick-up, soccer and ballet, and homework, Camila was very clear about the impossibility of planning and preparing meals during the week. She adamantly told me that there were not enough hours in her day and drive-through food outlets were the only way she could feed her family without losing her mind. What she did agree to was to keep a Log that specifically included the start and end times of driving to/from food pickups.

Camila arrived at my office the following week flabbergasted. She realized that her 'time-saving' strategy of drive-through food was costing her close to two hours each day. For a weekend investment of ½ hour planning and an hour trip to the supermarket for supplies, she could throw easy-to-assemble dinners in the oven for about 30 minutes after work while she caught her breath and chatted with the children about their day.

The happy result was two-fold. Camila found it much easier to lose the excess weight that had been a 'gift' of the fast-food conglomerates, and she noticed the children were more relaxed, completed homework with fewer complaints, and more easily transitioned into bedtime mode.

Must I keep a Behavior Log?

No. You can simply keep a Log. In fact, you may keep a journal, diary, self-monitoring form, register, account, chart, or record. Call it whatever you wish but *track your behavior*. Going forward, I will refer to this as your Log.

As you move toward your weight management goals, tracking your behaviors and their consequences is how you will identify the triggers behind your successes and your slips, as well as how to fine-tune your strategies to make things easier for yourself.

Marta

I met Marta when she was 57. Having become a little overweight during high school, she began a lifetime of dieting and arrived in my office seriously obese. She had been on every existing commercial weight loss plan in the US between the 20th and 21st centuries, as well as countless magazine, book, TV, and internet diets. For almost 40 years Marta had been trying to ignore her hunger and taste preferences to force herself into rigid, and sometimes bizarre (recall the cabbage diet? Urp.) regimens. She did lose weight with many of them and regained more than she lost with every single one. When Marta began working with me, she was at her highest weight, eating very light breakfasts and lunches, reasonable dinners, and snacking through the evening. The more weight she gained, the smaller her breakfasts and lunches became.

The first two things I asked Marta to do were start keeping a Log and increase the amount of food she ate during the day. We upped her intake for breakfast and lunch and added an afternoon snack. Convinced she would gain no fewer than a bazillion pounds, Marta nonetheless agreed to give my strategy a try for two weeks. She also agreed to do *The Stomach Exercise* three times before our next appointment.

One week later, Marta returned to my office with three copies of her completed *Stomach Exercise*, seven days of food records, and a whole lot of anxiety about stepping on the scale. Much to her delight, Marta had lost a few pounds during the week. By increasing her intake in the first part of the day, she had unwittingly decreased her evening snacking (we could see this in her Log) and ended up eating less than if she had continued to 'diet' during the day.

When we turned to Marta's *Stomach Exercise* forms, she expressed frustration at how difficult it was to identify physical cues of satiety. What we figured out is that, for Marta, satiety cues were simply the gradual disappearance of hunger cues (in her case, cold hands and noisy belly). Most surprising to her was the fact that long before she had consumed everything on her generously-laden plate, she really was not hungry anymore.

What should I Log?

There are many things that successful weight managers record depending on their unique situations and as you move forward, what you track will change depending on what you need to focus on at the time. Minimally, however, your record for each day should include the time you eat, what you eat, and how much of each food. There is no need to obsessively measure and weigh your food. No doubt you have followed plenty of diets that required you do that, so you are pretty good at eyeballing portions and knowing whether you are serving yourself a cup or a gallon, three ounces or three pounds.

Along with what and when you eat, include a brief note about any intake behavior that is excessive, stressful, or about which you are particularly proud. Having that context will prove invaluable when you need to figure out what is and is not working for you.

Action Item

Start a Log in which you record your food intake. For each day, have columns in which to record the time you eat, as well as what and how much you eat. In addition, include a 'context' column for notes about what is going on at the time if the eating episode is excessive, unplanned, or in any way noteworthy.

Refer to *Appendix—Sample Log* for an example of how my patients and I usually set up Logs. You can use this as a template or design your own. There are also many smartphone apps you can use to track your behavior but be careful to not pick one that pushes you toward any particular diet plan or product purchase. Your Log is supposed to support your personal goals, not someone else's financial goals!

What if I hate Logging?

In addition to logging your food intake, it will be important that you also record other behaviors and reactions.

Engaging in the physical act of recording your thoughts and behaviors serves four powerful functions: (1) It actively focuses you on the question at hand, (2) The physical act of recording promotes memory encoding so you are more likely to recall the information when you need it, (3) Having recorded the information, it is easily at hand if you need reminding, and (4) Research has indisputably confirmed that our memory for personal actions such as food intake, exercise, and emotional responses is easily distorted by all manner of things so a physical record is the only way to have accurate data of our behavior over time.

If you hate writing and are willing to write nonetheless, I am fairly certain you will discover that it becomes less annoying as you get used to it, and that it is helpful to achieving your goals.

If you hate writing and are unwilling to give it a try, then minimally promise yourself to pay attention to your process. When asked to write, make it a point to allocate a few minutes to actively focus on those topics and think them through as if you were writing. The investment will pay off handsomely.

POURING THE CEMENT

For your foundation to withstand the dramatic temperature changes the seasons bring, the material with which it is made must be high quality. In terms of weight management, this means that the way you think about things must be clear and logical.

Is my thinking the problem?

Your weight is the result of multiple forces, some intrinsic to your DNA, others to your environment, and still others due to how you think (talk to yourself) about your life. In this sense, your thinking is *part of* the problem.

We each have unique ways of thinking about the world and making sense of our experience. For the most part, our brains are terrifically effective at successfully interpreting our circumstances and making good decisions. To most efficiently process the multitude of information that comprises a life, we develop *thinking habits* (also called *automatic thoughts* or *self-talk*). While these habits are mostly very useful, they sometimes distort our ability to see things clearly and draw productive conclusions. For instance, someone whose typical thinking style is to see the negative side of things—the proverbial glass half empty person— is more likely to see small errors as catastrophic.

Thinking habits that get in the way of our happiness and productivity are called *cognitive distortions* or *cognitive errors*.

What cognitive distortions interfere with weight management?

The distortions I see most often among patients who struggle to manage their weight are as follows.

Catastrophizing—exaggerating the negative potential of an event despite little or no evidence that a catastrophic outcome is likely. For instance, the person who is working on establishing an exercise routine would interpret a missed workout as evidence of failure and may then be likely give up altogether.

Dichotomous thinking—tendency to see the world in black or white (or good or bad, on or off) terms rather than appreciating the infinite degrees of continuity between the extremes. The most common instance of this among dieters is interpreting a single lapse in plan adherence as evidence one has blown it and is off the plan altogether.

Emotional reasoning—assuming that one's emotional state or reaction is an accurate reflection of reality. The prototypical example of this causing trouble is not 'feeling' slimmer despite having lost weight, and concluding that the weight loss is not at all discernable and so the effort is pointless.

Over-generalizing—using narrow evidence to draw broad conclusions. For example, the person who over-generalizes is likely to conclude he is a total failure if he fails to achieve his weight management objectives, even if he is a rock star in other aspects of his life.

Disqualifying the positive—tendency to discount positive things about oneself, one's behavior, or one's circumstances. This causes an over-focus on the negative and, more often than not, results in discouragement and sadness. A common example is the person who makes significant improvements to her lifestyle but insists they are no big deal or just lucky breaks, and thus fails to benefit from the motivation that comes from feeling a sense of accomplishment.

How do I fix cognitive distortions?

The first step is to figure out which, if any, of the distortions you tend to use and when you most often do so. (You will do this in the next Action Item.) Once you know what distortions most often trip you up, develop ***rational rebuttals*** for each one. A rational rebuttal is the corrective explanation you would give a loved one who was upsetting him- or herself with these distortions. Since your version of the distortions is unique to you, and each situation in which you use it shapes its precise content, I cannot give you exact words to use. The best I can do is offer examples.

Catastrophizing—Juan weighed himself every Tuesday morning. On Tuesdays when the scale did not register weight loss, his reflex was to tell himself he is never going to achieve his goal, trying is hopeless, and he ought to give up! His ***rational rebuttal*** reminds him that he has been pretty consistent at making meaningful changes and has in fact been losing weight. He reminds himself that the lifestyle and physical improvements accomplished thus far are valuable in themselves, and the fact that he has made them happen is hard evidence that he is moving forward.

Dichotomous thinking—Marta enjoyed forward progress for several months before she and her husband vacationed at an all-inclusive resort. Upon arrival, they were greeted with a welcome bag of chocolate-dipped fruits and nuts which Marta and her husband enjoyed as they unpacked and settled in. As the last of the unexpected snacks disappeared, Marta found herself panicking that she had blown it, fallen off her plan! Her ***rational rebuttal*** entailed correcting the faulty thought that the lapse meant she was done. She told herself, "Slipping is inevitable and only means I'm human. I am usually consistent in my efforts and mistakes do not mean I've quit. In fact, I can use this situation to do some planning for the rest of the vacation where there will surely be other tricky situations. I can manage my enjoyment of vacation treats while maintaining as much as I can of my usual food and exercise routine."

Emotional reasoning—Having shaped her lifestyle to maintain a healthy weight range, Louise was fairly pleased with herself and the look and feel of her body. However, every month during her menstrual period, she would feel bloated as she retained water (perfectly normal for a healthy woman!). That bigger feeling triggered Louise to question whether she really was as healthy and attractive as she usually feels. Then she would decide that those good feelings were just delusions and she actually does look as terrible as she feels right now. Her ***rational rebuttal*** is fairly simple, "Feelings are not accurate reflections of reality. I feel big but that doesn't mean I am big. I am healthy-weighted and living a good life."

Over-generalizing—As a competent businesswoman raising healthy happy children, Camila was a success by any reasonable standards. However, to her way of thinking, the fact that she had been unable to manage her weight made her feel like a failure. Developing a ***rational rebuttal*** took a fair bit of work as Camila had grown up in a family that prioritized women's appearance over almost everything. Ultimately, she was able to boil down our many conversations to this: "It makes no more sense to label myself a failure because of one aspect of my life than it would to call my kids losers because of one poor grade, or my business a bust because of one bad sales month. In fact, the evidence is clear that I am kicking butt in most areas of my life. Needing help with my weight does not mean that I am a failure. It means I am not perfect—only human. Further, being smart enough to recognize I need help and seek it out is evidence of my competence!"

Disqualifying the positive—Hannah was one of those people who could easily create order out of chaos. Despite smoothly making the transition from an obesogenic lifestyle to one that promotes a healthy body, she continued to struggle with inter-mittent emotionally-driven lapses. When these occurred, Hannah would beat herself up for being ineffective. When I would point out that she was exceptionally effective in other areas, she would counter by stating those things are easy and do not count. (This is very similar to over-generalizing.) Hannah's **rational rebuttal** entailed reminding herself that the fact that something comes easily to her does not mean it is meaningless, so she would tell herself, "The things I easily do are difficult for others; they are signs of my competence," and then she would stop whatever she was doing (for a few seconds) and list three things she does well to remind herself to retain a balanced outlook.

Action Item

Pay attention to your emotional responses, and when you become upset or frustrated, think about your thinking. Is a **cognitive distortion** skewing your interpretation of the event? Script your **rational rebuttal** by thinking about what you would tell a loved one who was thinking and reacting the same way. Make note of the cognitive distortion, your actual self-talk, and the rational rebuttal in the Context column of your Log. Refer to these notes when you find yourself in similar emotional situations down the road.

What is mindless eating?

Let us start with what mindless eating is *not*. It is not eating without thinking. Your mind (brain) is always active—even when it seems to have left the room. Mindless eating is how we describe eating that feels automatic or unconscious because you are responding to cues on which you are not actively focused.

For instance, you settle down to watch a movie beside your friend who has brought a large bucket of hot, buttery popcorn. You thoroughly enjoy the movie and as the closing credits roll, realize you have eaten much more popcorn than intended. What happened is that you were attending to two sets of cues. One was the movie that you intentionally watched. The other set of cues was the connection between the sight and smell of food and your genetic predisposition to eat when food is present. With your intentional concentration focused on the movie, your primitive reflex kicked in.

There is not really anything we can do about our genetics, but you most certainly can improve your ability to recognize and manage cues that trigger mindless responses; and that begins with recognizing your high-risk situations.

What are high-risk situations?

High-risk situations (HRS) are circumstances that easily trigger you to act out of alignment with your plans and goals. If you were trying to quit smoking, an HRS would be spending the evening in a smoke-filled nightclub; that would put you at risk for slipping. Similarly, if you need to do well on an important exam and decide to study in the park where your friends are horsing around, ... well, you get the picture.

High-risk situations can roughly be divided into those that are external to ourselves (e.g., hot buttery popcorn) and those that are internal such as thoughts, mood, and physical sensations.

All of us are susceptible to both external and internal HRS for overeating. Some people are significantly more susceptible to external triggers, others to internal, and most of us respond to a mix of both. As you progress through this book you will learn many strategies to lessen the power of your HRS. First, however, it is helpful to think about whether you have a particular weakness for one type of HRS over another.

External HRS are those aspects of your environment that trigger you to start or to continue eating regardless of physical hunger. Examples include the sight or smell of food, the time of day, other people eating or offering you food, food advertisements, and social events. If you find it difficult not to overeat in these situations, even when you are not hungry, then external triggers are a serious challenge for you and the chapter on **Environment & Hunger** will be especially important for you.

Internal HRS run the gamut of what goes on within the confines of your body. Although physical hunger signals are not necessarily HRS, if your frequent reaction to them is one of *overeating*, you may need to rethink how you structure your eating patterns as well as the settings in which you eat. In this case, both **Environment & Hunger**, and **Food & Hunger** will need your attention. Internal HRS also encompass emotions and thought patterns. Thought patterns that interfere with your ability to effectively manage your weight are addressed throughout the book as, clearly, your thoughts determine what you do. Emotions may well be the most difficult HRS to get a handle on as they can be overwhelming. Nonetheless, people do learn to manage them. **Emotions & Hunger** will help you get the upper hand on these HRS.

Louise

Louise was a young attorney quickly working her way to partner in a prestigious law firm. She was used to coming first in her classes, receiving promotions quickly, and generally winning at almost everything she put her mind to—except weight management. She had gained weight during adolescence and then lost and regained it several times during college. Louise told me that she had no trouble getting started losing weight but never managed to stay with any plan long enough to hit her goal. After we adjusted her goal to something more realistic than what she had weighed at age 14(!), Louise began to keep a Log. What quickly became apparent was that she had little trouble following her plans most of the time but when she deviated at all, she spiraled. In other words, when she made a mistake, she reflexively told herself that she had blown it and ... what the heck. From there, the rest of the day or the week or the whole objective was lost to her.

The solution for Louise was twofold. First, she had to come to grips with the fact that not everything in life will come easily to her and this truth did not mean she was an unsuccessful person. It meant simply that she is a person, a human. Simple as this sounds, it took a fair bit of talking and thinking for Louise to really believe it in her gut but gradually she became comfortable with the idea. In fact, she reported this gave her a sense of freedom that she had not previously felt. The second thing that helped Louise get a better handle on her eating behavior was identifying (from her Log) the types of situations that were most likely to trip her up. Her most common high-risk situation was unexpected social meals. On days that she had either brought a lunch or planned her at-home dinner and found herself going out with colleagues or friends, she inevitably overate and then threw in the towel on the rest of her self-care plans.

Action Item

To start yourself on the path of gaining mastery over your **high-risk situations**, identify two or three situations that have repeatedly triggered overeating in the past and start paying attention when they occur and how you respond to them. If you have not already done so, **add a Place/Doing column to your Log**. Recording where and/or what you are doing while eating, along with other notes in the Context column will help you identify and manage high-risk situations as you move forward.

Why do most diets fail?

Most diets do not fail. As long as the diet results in a caloric deficit (that is, you eat fewer calories than you burn), you lose weight. Assuming no significant underlying medical conditions, there are two reasons people either do not lose weight on diets or do not maintain their losses.

First, following an eating plan designed by someone who is not living your life is like forcing yourself to wear the wrong size shoes because you love the color. You might be able to squeeze into them and hobble about for a bit, but ultimately you are going to kick the painful things off. Same goes for following other people's diets. You might be able to suck it up and live on cabbage for a week or a month or so, but unless you were born LOVING cabbage, ultimately you are going to toss the diet in the trash. So, if you want to lose weight and not regain it, eat a wide variety of foods you enjoy in quantities that result in a slight caloric reduction. As your weight drops, if you have not reduced your caloric intake too severely (see **Chapter 6—Food & Hunger**), you will become comfortable with the smaller portions and your weight will stabilize nicely without further restriction.

In addition to adopting diets that do not fit their lifestyle, the other reason people do not stick with their weight-management eating plans is something I call the **What-the-Heck-Effect**. It is the phenomenon of trying to be super-good on your diet, slipping up, saying "What the heck!", and giving up. Instead of acknowledging the fact that you are human and bound to mess up at times, you give up and that is the end of that. And you regain weight.

What-the-Heck Effect?

While you may not recognize the label, you know the experience. You set out to follow a diet (or quit smoking or never again bite your nails or …) and you slip. Upset by it, you tell yourself, "I've failed, what the heck" and you give up. As a result, in the diet scenario what could have been one regretted decision turns into a free-fall into weight gain. (By the way, this is an example of the cognitive distortion of catastrophizing.)

In the psychology literature this process is called the *Abstinence Violation Effect*[1] and was first discussed in the context of alcohol and drug abuse. It describes what happens when someone has set an abstinence rule such as 'get on the wagon and never drink again' but slips and has a drink. Having broken the rule, the individual concludes she or he has 'fallen off the wagon' and resumes drinking.

Obviously, you are not getting on the abstinence wagon from food. If you did, you would die. Nonetheless, this phenomenon applies to those goals or rules you set for yourself that allow no space to be human. If your plan is to do everything I recommend perfectly all the time, one microscopic deviation can send you off the deep edge.

Can I avoid the What-the Heck Effect?

Yes. The first thing to do is accept the fact that you are going to slip. Unless you are an alien from a galaxy nothing like ours, you are not perfect. Nothing about your appearance can be perfect, nothing about your thinking can be perfect, and nothing about your behavior can be perfect. You can be pretty darn good—but NOT PERFECT!

Changing behavior is hard. Every time you reach for an extra cookie or sleep late rather than get on the treadmill, there are countless factors that push you toward each decision. Each slip gives you a wonderful opportunity to learn a little more about what makes you tick. With that knowledge, you can turn your slips into strengths and avoid the What-the-Heck Effect.

How do I turn slips into strengths?

Turning a slip into a strength requires you to **Contextualize, Plan, and Rehearse (CPR).**

First, you must examine in detail the Context of the slip. Look closely at everything about the situation and everything about what you did and thought in the situation so that you have as detailed a picture as possible. The more aware you are of all the big and little triggers, the more power you will have over them.

To fully **Contextualize** the slip, answer questions one through four about the situation and questions five through 12 about your response to it:

1. Where were you, and when was it?
2. How were you feeling physically, emotionally?
3. What was on your mind?

4. Who were you with, and what did that person (those people) say or do that affected you?

5. What did you say to yourself?

6. What did you feel?

7. Did your feelings change as the situation unfolded? If yes, how?

8. How did you expect to *feel right away if you gave in* to the temptation?

9. How did you expect to *feel later if you gave in* now?

10. How did you expect to *feel right away if you said no* to the temptation?

11. How did you expect to *feel later if you said no* to the temptation?

12. What did you do just before you gave in?

Create a summary of your answers and when you have a pretty good picture of what triggered you to abandon your self-care plans, explore other ways you can handle similar situations in the future. To devise a better plan, think about aspects of the situation itself that you might be able to modify or eliminate next time, and what actions and thoughts of your own that can be modified. It helps to think about this process as writing a script of what happened based on your answer to the Context questions, then revising the script with healthier actions and thoughts so that similar future circumstances do not trigger lapses. In other words, script a **Plan**.

Finally, **Rehearse** your plan. In your mind's eye, reconstruct the situation as you contextualized it and imagine yourself responding with your new script.

Louise's CPR

Here is how Louise, the young attorney who repeatedly overate whenever she dined out with friends, came up with a workable strategy to enjoy meeting up with friends without overeating.

Contextualize:

1. At Ernesto's Mexican Restaurant right after work.
2. I was in a good mood, happy to be meeting friends for dinner. Well, maybe a tiny bit nervous because of my history of overeating when I go out.
3. Arguing with myself whether I should cancel and stick to my eating plan or go out and blow it.
4. With three friends, all talking about how Ernesto's has the best enchiladas and sopapillas in town and how hungry we all were. The more they raved about the food, the sorrier I felt for myself that I wouldn't, or at least shouldn't, get to eat it all.
5. I told myself it wasn't fair that I had to watch my intake and who was I kidding anyhow, I knew I was going to blow it so what's the use.
6. Lousy.
7. I started the meal feeling both bad about myself and happy to be enjoying all that awesome food. By the end of the meal, all I felt was stuffed and ashamed.
8. Hmmm ... to be honest, I didn't think about how I would feel right away if I gave in to temptation.
9. Didn't think about how I would feel later either.
10. I knew I would feel deprived if I didn't order as much as my friends did.
11. Never gave a thought to how I would feel later that evening if I ordered less than my friends and had only one sopapilla.

12. I cannot remember anything about the moment just
before I gave in!

Summarize the Context. I approach going out to eat with
friends from a lose/lose perspective. Either I will choose
quantities that move me toward my goals and feel deprived,
or order quantities I love and feel guilty—either way, I lose.
So, having set myself up to feel lousy, I tell myself that
it's not fair I have to pay attention to my intake and I'm
hopeless at controlling myself anyhow and I may as well
just order the extra-large everything. And, without giving it
a second thought, I do. And then I hate myself.

Explore my options and creating a Plan. I do not want to
change the fact that I go out with friends so that's off the
table, nor do I want Ernesto's to be off-limits. Obviously, I
cannot force my friends not to talk about how hungry they
are or how good the food is. That leaves me with modifying
my self-talk and my actions. To start, I need to change my
thinking from lose/lose to how do I make this work for me?
I am learning to accept the fact that I am not perfect, and
it is just nuts to expect myself always to follow my plans
exactly. So, the first step in my plan is to approach the event
with the thought that I can enjoy my friends and enjoy
delicious food just as well without super-sizing the whole
thing. As for the pity party about how unfair it is that I
have to watch my intake, well, that certainly needs revising.
I think that once I remind myself that enchiladas taste just
as good if you have one serving instead of two, I will feel
a little less sorry for myself. Further, I can remind myself
that it is also nuts to expect to always get everything I want.
Fulfilling my 'want' to live at a healthier weight means I
don't get to fulfil my 'want' for large portions. So, step two
will be telling myself that the single portion is giving me
what I really want in my life. Finally, during this decision

process, I need to remind myself how I will feel later if I supersize my meal (lousy) and how I will feel later if I do not. Obviously, if I resist the urge to over-order, later I will be proud of myself instead of feeling guilty. When I see the waiter coming to take our orders, I will imagine myself enjoying a healthy portion of delicious food and feeling like a winner as I pay the bill.

Rehearse the new script. Daily for the next few days, and then at least three times on the way to my next dinner with friends, I will imagine the following: Happily joining friends at the restaurant and thinking how grateful I am to have good friends and the ability to enjoy good food at the same time I take care of my health. Ernesto's (or wherever we're meeting) food tastes just as good in single as multiple portions so I am going to enjoy it tremendously and feel really good about myself while doing so. If I feel tempted to over-order, I will remind myself that doing so will ruin the evening for me and ordering a healthy portion will taste delicious and feel terrific. Then I will place my order and enjoy my time with friends.

Action Item

Pick one or two of the high-risk situations you identified earlier and ***practice applying CPR*** to them. As you go forward, keep an eye on your Log for circumstances (settings, activities, emotions) that repeatedly cause you trouble and apply CPR to each one.

HARDENING THE CEMENT

To ensure your foundation is able to weather whatever the elements throw at it, you must allow it to fully harden before stomping around on it. For weight management purposes, this means not sabotaging yourself by setting inappropriate weight goals.

How much should I weigh?

The first thing you need to know is that your body has its limits. It is not infinitely modifiable. Despite advertisers who promise the body you want if you buy their products, the truth is that your body has a somewhat fixed range of size and shape within which it can exist. If you have always been relatively heavy, chances are slim that you will ever be especially thin for any extended length of time. Similarly, if you have always been quite thin, odds are against you being able to achieve great obesity without working extremely hard to do so.

The second thing you need to know is that your body is a living, fluctuating organism. Thus, setting a specific, single-number weight goal is ridiculous. You cannot weigh the exact same number every day forever. Setting a target *weight range*, on the other hand, is reasonable. Moreover, if that range is realistic for your biology and lifestyle, it will help you achieve your goals rather than create frustration which invariably leads to defeat. (Plus, if you are an emotional over-eater, chasing the depressingly frustrating weight will make you heavier.)

There are two things to consider in deciding on an appropriate target weight range. One is guidance from medical science and the other is your reality.

What is my healthy weight range?

Medical science[2] discusses body weight in terms of a weight to height ratio called Body Mass Index (BMI). You can look up your BMI online, or calculate your BMI with the following formula:

$$(\text{Pounds} \times 703)/\text{inches}^2) = BMI$$

Example: Clara weighs 187 pounds and is 64 inches tall $\rightarrow$

$$(187 \times 703)/64^2 = 131,461/4,096 = 32.09$$

The **Weight Categories Table** below shows you what BMI values fall into Underweight, Healthy Weight, Overweight, and Obese categories. Clara's BMI places her in the Obese category.

Waist circumference is also a factor in determining your medical risk. For men, waists that measure more than 40 inches add risk, and for women waistlines more than 35 inches increase the risk for illness. Weights outside of the Healthy Weight range are associated with health risks; as your weight moves from overweight to increasing degrees of obesity, and your waistline expands, your health risk increases. Similarly, dropping below Healthy Weight carries added risk to your health.

Weight Categories	
	BMI
Underweight	Under 18.5
Healthy Weight	18.5 to 24.9
Overweight	25.0 to 29.9
Obese	30 and over

As you consider your optimal BMI range, it is important to understand that science provides general guidelines for 'generic' people. In other words, they are reasonable rules of thumb to consider but not equally applicable to everyone. For instance, if you are a heavily muscled body builder, you may have a high BMI but not necessarily have elevated health risk because all that muscle adds pounds without adding the negatives of excess fat. If your physician has recommended a particular weight range that is optimal for your unique physical reality, do not worry about fitting yourself on the BMI table. *However!* If your doc has prescribed a target weight for you, be sure to translate that prescription into a weight *range*. Regardless of the source of your target, you are still a living organism so aiming for one single number is as effective as shooting yourself in the foot to help you run faster.

With these considerations in mind, you can now compare your BMI with those shown in the table. If your BMI falls within the Healthy Weight range, and there are no medical reasons for you to alter it, I encourage you to enjoy the body you have and focus on providing it with good nutrition and pleasurable exercise. If your BMI falls into the Underweight range and you have pretty much always been on the light side, as long as you are strong and healthy, there is no reason to focus on changing your weight. However, if you have only recently fallen below a healthy range, make sure this is not a sign either of illness (see your physician), or an eating disorder (see ***Do I have an eating disorder?***)

If your BMI falls into the Overweight or Obese ranges, your next step will be to blend this bit of scientific guidance with the reality of your personal biology into a target range that you can achieve.

How do I blend science and personal biology into a target I can hit?

The way to figure out where *your* best target weight range lies is by considering both your *Family Profile* and *Personal Weight Inventory*.

To illustrate this process, I will show you how 34-year-old Clara arrived at her target weight range, and then walk you through figuring out your own best target range.

To build her *Family Profile*, Clara did two things. First, she used the following grid to capture the weight status of her family, placing an X for each individual in the relevant column. For example, Clara placed an X under 'healthy weight' for her father and an X under 'overweight/obese' for her mother, one X under 'healthy weight' for one of her siblings and two Xs under 'overweight/obese" for the other two, and so on. Then, she totaled the number of X's in each column. Note that for this step, we combine overweight and obese because it is unlikely Clara, or you, will know the exact weights of family members—but it is easy to eyeball whether someone appears generally healthy-weighted versus not.

Clara's Family Profile—Step 1			
	Underweight	Healthy Weight	Overweight/ Obese
Parents		X	X
Siblings		X	XX
Grandparents		X	XXX
Aunts/Uncles/Cousins		XXX	XXXXX
Totals:	0	6	11

To make the result easier to see, Clara then converted the information into a simple chart as follows. As you can see, Clara's genetic inheritance is shared with almost twice as many people who fall into the overweight/obese category as fall into the healthy category.

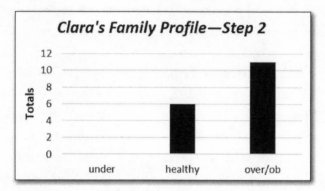

Clara then documented her **Personal Weight Inventory** by placing an X in the column that best describes her weight at each age timeframe in the following table.

Clara's Personal Weight Inventory				
Age	Underweight	Healthy Weight	Overweight	Obese
0–5 years		X		
6–10 years		X		
11–15 years		X		
16–20 years			X	
21–25 years			X	
26–30 years			X	
31–35 years				X

Clara's **Personal Weight Inventory** tells us that she has been overweight most of her adult life, and only recently moved into the obese range. Given this scenario, targeting a low weight in the healthy range would likely set Clara up for frustration and disappointment. While it is possible that both her and her family's overweight/obese status is entirely due to unhealthy habits, it is more likely that genetics play a role as well. Hence, the sensible thing for Clara to do is to set a target in the overweight range, which is very likely achievable and will result in a reduction of medical risk as well. In the future, if maintaining that target range is easy, she can work on reducing further. For now, though, setting too low a target will most likely land her in the old territory of lose and regain.

For Clara's height of 64 inches, overweight is defined as between 145 and 174 pounds. Although at her current weight of 187 pounds Clara would need to lose 13 pounds to achieve the overweight category, she has decided to strive for the lower end of that category and set her target range at 145–155 pounds. When she achieves this, if she finds it relatively easy to maintain and wants to reduce further, she can at that point shift the range lower. In the meantime, however, this is an achievable objective and will certainly result in a positive change to both her appearance and her health.

To figure out your own best target range, complete Steps 1 and 2 of your *Family Profile* as we did for Clara.

Family Profile—Step 1			
Place X's in the relevant columns for each family member.			
	Underweight	Healthy Weight	Overweight/ Obese
Parents			
Siblings			
Grandparents			
Aunts/Uncles/Cousins			
Totals:			

Stack the total number of X's from Step 1 in the corresponding weight categories in Step 2. The weight category with the tallest stack of X's gives you an idea of your likely genetic loading. (Note that I only included a possible total of 15 per category. If you have many more relatives than that, simply make the graph taller and enjoy the pleasures of a large family!)

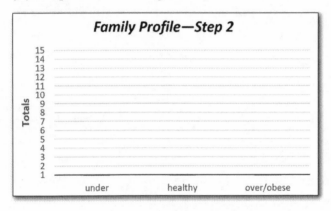

Next, complete your ***Personal Weight Inventory***. If you recall your weight category changing during any of the age brackets, either place the X for that age bracket under the category that corresponds to the one you were in for most of that period, or place an X in both categories if that makes more sense.

Personal Weight Inventory				
Place X's to indicate your weight category during each age range.				
Age	Underweight	Healthy Weight	Overweight	Obese
0–5 years				
6–10 years				
11–15 years				
16–20 years				
21–25 years				

Personal Weight Inventory				
Place X's to indicate your weight category during each age range.				
Age	Underweight	Healthy Weight	Overweight	Obese
26–30 years				
31–35 years				
36–40 years				
41–45 years				
46–50 years				
51–55 years				
56–60 years				
61+				

Action Item

Consider the information you have just organized, think about how much weight you have been able to lose and keep off over the past 10 years, and then *select a target 10-pound range that makes sense*. For instance:

- If you come from a predominantly overweight and obese family and have been obese yourself for most of your adult life, start with a target of 20 or 30 pounds less than you weigh now, and define your range as that number plus/minus five pounds. For example, if you currently weigh 220 pounds, target 200 or 190, and then set the range as either 195–205 or 185–195.

- If your family is mostly healthy-weighted and you've only become overweight during the past few years, set your target for within the healthy category, plus/minus five pounds. For example, if the healthy range for your height is 114 to 144 and you currently weigh 160, set your target range for 130–140 pounds.

How important is it to get my range right?

Not especially important—as long as you do not set it too low. Targeting a weight range that is too far below what your **Family Profile** and **Personal Weight Inventory** suggest is achievable will result either in you giving up well before you get there, or getting there only to quickly rebound and regain.

Why a range instead of a specific weight?

Easy question—because you are alive. You can no more weigh exactly the same every day as you can have a good hair day every day. Your body weight fluctuates naturally over time, even if it remains within a fairly stable range. So, a target *range* is achievable and maintainable.

A specific weight will slip into and out of your grasp as easily as your hair is wind-blown. If you are like most of us, the disappointment when you see that number change can make you question whether the effort is worth it. When that happens, we often retire from trying, revert to old behaviors, and regain. A range, on the other hand, allows you to see the success in weighing X today, perhaps X minus 2 tomorrow, and X plus 2 the next day—all within your comfort zone.

How wide a range makes sense?

There is no one right answer for this. A lot depends on how your body reacts to life and how overweight you are. A reasonable starting point, though, is targeting a range of about five to 10 pounds. As you get used to the behaviors that get you into that range, you may find it becomes easier to narrow the range.

However, beware of slipping into the trap of thinking that because for the past few days, or weeks, or months your weight has stayed in a very narrow range that it must always be there. Undoubtedly, there will be periods during which your weight will fluctuate more broadly; this should trigger you to review your behavior but not to conclude that you have blown it.

Action Item

Just in case you ignored that last Action Item, I am encouraging you again. Resist the temptation to say, "Oh I already know what I should/want to weigh" and skip using the **Personal Weight Profile**. While you may be right, you may also be wrong; or if not wrong, sufficiently off to set yourself up for unnecessary frustration. It will take only a few minutes to complete the Profile. **Do it. Now.**

Can medication help?

Over the past century a variety of medications have taken center stage as the great new cure for overeating and obesity. Some are appetite suppressants or satiety- or metabolism-enhancers, and some interfere with fat (calorie) absorption. Still others promise to dissolve your fat or make you no longer like sweets. To a degree, a few actually do what they are advertised to. However, not a single one has produced lasting effects. Appetite eventually returns, people are able to eat even when not hungry, extended periods of quickened metabolism ultimately turn toxic, and the list of disappointments goes on.

So, the answer to the question "Can drugs help?" is "Maybe a little." If your physician recommends using an FDA-approved medication to assist with weight loss, you may find it helpful to kick-start your weight management efforts. **However!** If you believe that medication will *solve* your overeating problem, I guarantee you will be sorely disappointed, as well as be out a chunk of change in drug costs. Whether using meds or having surgery or attending an expensive 'health camp', weight management comes down to you doing two things: (1) Deciding that healthy weight is a priority, and (2) Making the commitment to adjust (not replace) your lifestyle to support that priority. Medication can temporarily help things move a little more quickly but ultimately it will always come back to you doing the work. (Sorry if that was not the answer you were hoping for.)

What makes a successful weight manager?

That *National Weight Control Registry*[3] is a research database of over 10,000 people who have lost anywhere from 30 to over 300 pounds and kept it off for significant lengths of time. Established in 1994, the Registry has resulted in many important findings about people who are able to successfully get the upper hand on their weight. As you might expect, with information from over 10,000 individuals, there is a lot of variety in the how and when of their methods. However, there are some important across-the-board commonalities that you should know.

- There is close to a 50/50 split among those accomplishing their weight loss objectives on their own (45%) versus those doing so with the help of a program (55%). So, use the method that feels right for you, and if you start down one path that proves too rocky, switch! It often takes people several attempts until they figure out what works best for them, or whether they do best with a hybrid approach. The **Weight Loss Resume** you will develop in Chapter 4 can help you short-circuit some of the trial and error going forward.

- Almost every single individual (98%) in the Registry modified their food intake in some way to lose weight.

- Almost everyone (94%) increased their physical activity, and 90% exercise an average of one hour each day.

FOUNDATION ROUNDUP

First and foremost, if you have or suspect you have an eating disorder (ED), consult a mental health professional and work on resolving the ED before trying to change your weight. Getting the ED under control will make everything else easier.

We have explored the disconnect between our biology and the environmental forces that shape our behavior. Hopefully, you have taken seriously my suggestion to really think about the differences between your 21st Century lifestyle and that of the primitive ancestors whose DNA you carry. The difference in amount of physical exertion required to put dinner on your table versus that of your ancestors is dramatic. You now understand that the DNA of which you are built is primed to drive more food intake and higher body weight in our food-rich environment than it would in our native one. Further, one of the effects of this DNA is that we easily become deaf to body signals of hunger and satiety leaving us with little on which to base our eating decisions other than environmental cues. Completing the *Stomach Exercise* is the first step toward learning to recognize and ultimately be able to use your own body signals to moderate the impact of the environment.

We have also talked about ***cognitive distortions*** and how thinking patterns skew your interpretation of events to cause negative emotional reactions that, in turn, interfere with your ability to achieve your goals. Begin working on ***rational rebuttals*** to keep moving forward.

Give particular attention to the cognitive distortion of catastrophizing which triggers the ***What the Heck Effect***. Unless today is your very first-ever effort at behavior change, I know this experience is familiar to you. Take that emotional leap to accept your imperfect self and shift your perspective to seeing slips as opportunities to learn more about how to self-manage. Applying ***CPR*** to past slips is one of the most effective ways to make that happen. This may turn out to be one of the most powerful things you do on this journey.

Along with being on the lookout for troublesome cognitive distortions, watch for situations that repeatedly interfere with maintaining your focus. These ***high-risk situations*** include cognitive distortions, but also include physical and social triggers. ***Logging*** your behavior is the best way to identify and master these obstacles.

Finally, realistic, achievable goals are wonderfully helpful to all projects, including self-improvement ones. Unfortunately, most dieters actually sabotage themselves by setting weight goals that make no sense for their unique bodies and lifestyles. Having completed your ***Family Profile*** and ***Personal Weight Inventory*** to identify a target weight range will make it easier for you to stick with the behaviors that promote weight management.

Action Step Recap:

At this point if you are acting on all the Action Items, you will already have taken several steps towards achieving a livable healthy weight. To ensure you have not missed anything, here they are again:

1. Reflect on the amount of energy required for survival in our modern world, compared with that of our ancestors. Keep in mind that our bodies are designed for that primitive existence and so maintaining a healthy weight is not 'natural' for most of us and requires attention and effort. To overcome this obstacle, seek opportunities to **add movement to your daily routine**.

2. Improving your ability to recognize your body's signals of hunger and satiety will help you know when to start and when to stop eating. These signals are seldom very pronounced in most people and are decidedly difficult to perceive if you have spent years dieting. Do **The Stomach Exercise** three times over the course of a week. It will introduce you to your body's hunger language and make it easier to eat well without overeating.

3. Start paying attention to how you think. Watch for **cognitive distortions** and free yourself from their grip by scripting **rational rebuttals**.

4. Review past weight management efforts for those recurrent situations that trigger you to slip and abandon your plans. These are your **high-risk situations**. Being aware of them is the first step toward controlling their impact.

5. Complete the **Family Profile** and **Personal Weight Inventory** to determine your most reasonable target weight range. Doing so will dramatically increase the odds that you achieve your goal because it will make sense in the context of your unique biology and lifestyle.

6. ***Start a Log.*** Tracking your intake will in itself likely trigger a degree of reduced intake and hence weight loss. More critically, it will allow you to trouble-shoot when you trip on the inevitable obstacles in your path.

7. Using one or two of the high-risk situations you have identified, practice applying ***CPR***.

FOUNDATION FOR PARENTS

Our children learn what we live. No matter how articulate or compelling your lectures, your child will ultimately copy your actions. Indeed, research has demonstrated that even family members who are not actively involved in changing dietary patterns often end up experiencing a positive impact on their weight and wellbeing[4]

If you have implemented the recommendations in this chapter for yourself, you have already made an important difference in your child's likelihood of having a weight struggle. You are moving around a little more which subtly but meaningfully changes what your child is learning about what 'normal' is.

I do not recommend that you talk to your child about his or her weight. Doing so will be pointless if your child is too young to take control of his or her lifestyle, or toxic if old enough to become self-conscious about his or her body. If your child's body falls outside the normative size range, there is already plenty of cultural pressure to make him or her feel bad; home is where your child should feel 100% acceptable. Moreover, cultural body ideals are so exceedingly thin that even if your child is at a healthy weight, the pervasive message is that thinner is better. This is a recipe for eating disorders and eating disorders can kill.

I also encourage you to refrain from talking about your own

weight with, or in front of, your child. No matter how lovingly you describe your child's body, hearing mom or dad put down their own bodies sends the message that body size and shape are important and can be 'wrong.' Further, as your child develops into a man or woman, he or she begins to look more like mom or dad; if mom or dad is 'ugly' in any way, the only logical conclusion your child can draw is that he or she too is 'ugly.' Combine that with the extreme cultural ideals and the eating disorder recipe is super-charged.

Finally, with respect to your child's weight, if your pediatrician has expressed concern about it being too high, the best approach is to stop or slow weight gain and allow the child to grow into his or her weight. Do this by leading a more active lifestyle, ensuring there are ample fresh food choices in the home, and minimizing the amount of processed food (these are usually high-fat and/or high-sugar) available to the family. Taking charge of your own physical health will enhance that of your child.

CHAPTER 4

MOTIVATION

Dictionary.com defines motivation as "the state or condition of being motivated or having a strong reason to act or accomplish something." That makes it sound as though once you are motivated to do something, that motivation is something you *have*, and it is here to stay. Does that sound like your experience?

I thought not.

A more accurate definition is that motivation is a fluctuating state of readiness to take action[5]. This breaks down into three parts: (1) "fluctuating" means you might be fired up for something right now but in a week or month or even in a day or an hour, your fire may fizzle; (2) the "state of readiness" is your emotional connection to the reason for action; and (3) the "action" targets a goal.

Due to its ephemeral nature, we tend to think of motivation as one of those things we need but do not really have any control over. Hence, we forge ahead when we are feeling motivated and bemoan our lack of motivation when our efforts grind to a halt. What we fail to do is actively manage our motivation to maintain it, *and* plan for how to maintain our focus when motivation lags.

The trick to keeping ourselves moving toward our objectives is threefold. We must identify what it is that motivates us for a particular objective and make that feeling as tangibly real as we can. We must also identify and plan for those circumstances that are likely to throw us off our game. In other words, we must plan for the unplanned. Finally, we need to figure out how to move ahead even when motivation is low or absent.

Before going any further, I need to define the "*it*" in "identify what *it* is that motivates." Your chances of succeeding at lifelong weight management are best if you have multiple desires motivating you. Hence, the "*it*" of motivation is actually a mixed bag of multiple things that are important to you. As you work through this chapter, be generous and fill the bag with desires both large and small.

MAKE IT REAL

Owing to their intangible nature, emotional connections to motivating reasons are difficult to grab hold of. The answers provided here will add a concrete dimension to your motivation, making it easier to keep alive and call on when needed.

Are there good and bad motivations?

It is important to be honest with yourself about why you want to lose weight, and it is important to ensure those reasons work to your benefit. I would never go so far as to say that some motivations are 'bad,' but I will caution you that some are more likely to help and some more likely to disappoint. If your primary motivation is to please other people or change their responses to you, you may be setting yourself up for disappointment. No matter how loving and supportive (or punitive and demanding) the people you are trying to please are, you need to translate those reasons into personally meaningful ones (e.g., in addition to making my spouse happy, I want to be more fit and stronger so I can do more without needing help). If your reasons are not personal (unique to you), meaningful (relevant to your life), and make you feel something emotionally, your motivation is at the mercy of other people's moods, not to mention whether you are happy or miffed with them at the moment.

Why does my weight matter?

There are as many reasons people want to change their weight as there are people who want to do so. Over the years, patients have shared with me many reasons for pursuing weight management. Most reasons, however, can be sorted into roughly four categories. As you read through them, think about how each relates to you and try to include some component of each in your motivational bag.

Health—Medical science is very clear about the negative impact of excess weight. As you move from healthy weight (BMI of 18.5 to 24.9) to overweight (BMI of 25 to 29.9) to obesity (BMI ≥ 30), you face increased risk for development of diabetes, cardiovascular disease (e.g., high cholesterol, hypertension, heart attacks), certain cancers (e.g., colorectal, liver), sleep apnea, and fertility disorders. In addition to making you susceptible to ailments such as these, excess weight can contribute to fatigue and general feelings of physical discomfort. If health is a key motivator for you, my hope is that you are taking this step to avoid becoming ill. If you have already been diagnosed with an obesity-linked condition, I applaud you for taking this important step to enhance your health and your life.

Appearance—Almost everyone who is overweight believes

she or he will be more attractive if slimmer. Depending upon how overweight you are, weight loss may indeed improve your appearance. However, if changing your appearance is the only reason you are losing weight, there are a few things to keep in mind. One is that while weight loss will change your overall size, it will do little to change your basic shape. Weight loss *and* exercise may have an impact on your shape but in most cases will result in a smaller and firmer version of your current shape, and not in the media ideal you may be after. If you hold realistic expectations about the degree of change in appearance, you will likely find yourself more satisfied.

Interpersonal—Reasons in this category span the breadth of human interaction. Some people undertake weight loss to reduce a loved one's worry for them, or to impress someone. Others lose weight in order to feel more confident in social situations, enhance their social standing, or change the way co-workers or employers see them. However, be careful about unrealistic expectations as others do not necessarily react the way we expect them to, and the bottom line is that we cannot control their reactions. Hence, if changing your interpersonal dynamic is a key driver of your efforts, please think very carefully about how much of it is within your control (e.g., speaking up with confidence) versus outside your control (e.g., how others react) and focus on that which you can control.

Ability—Closely aligned with health reasons are those related to the abilities and activities excess weight interferes with. Many people undertake weight management when their size begins to interfere with the things they need to do or enjoy doing. For instance, greater ease playing with children or grandchildren, less difficulty climbing stairs or cleaning their home, greater stamina to dance the night away—you get the picture!

How big is my motivation?

That is a good question! It is also one that most people never think to ask, but one that left unanswered easily derails them. While most of us have no difficulty feeling strongly motivated to *have achieved* our goals, we are not always equally motivated to take the actions required *to achieve* them. There is a difference between wanting to weigh less and wanting to do the things needed to weigh less. If you love living exactly as you currently do and the thought of changing anything at all feels like tragic sacrifice, this may not be the best time to target weight loss.

What you may be more ready to do is change one small piece of the larger puzzle. For instance, perhaps you are ready to gently increase your physical stamina by adding a little more Natural Activity to your day. Or maybe you are finally ready to humor your doctor and include a few fruits and vegetables in your week. Perhaps learning a focused relaxation exercise to better handle stress and reduce stress eating appeals to you.

I suspect that even if the words "change your lifestyle" make you want to burn this book, somewhere in your mind is an idea of how your life might become better if you keep moving toward a healthier lifestyle. So, decide what goal, large or small, inspires you, or simply does not make you want to burn this book, and read on.

Action Item

Put down in writing exactly ***what* you hope to accomplish *and why***. For instance, you might state that you want to reduce your weight to the range of X to Y because it will reduce your risk for heart disease or help you feel more confident in social situations. Do not omit notating the *why* behind the *what*. As time moves forward and challenges arise, it will be important to remember why the goal matters. Do this for every motivating reason you have identified thus far and add new ones as they emerge.

How do I stay motivated?

First and foremost, invest time and energy right now to capture your motivation while you can feel it. In the space between the excitement that is driving you forward right now and the exhilaration you feel as you near the goal, there is a meandering path of neither here nor there. It is during the neither/nor time that you are at greatest risk of losing your drive and abandoning your efforts.

Today, you are in touch with how great you feel about doing something good for yourself. You are also vividly aware of how unhappy you feel about your current condition. Your insurance against dropping out is to capture today's feelings and save and savor them as you sail toward your destination. In a sense, this is like beginning a sailing trip with a good stiff wind filling your sails and capturing that wind in a bottle to use again and again whenever you need an extra push.

What is my first step?

Bottle your motivational wind!

If you tend to make emotional connections most strongly through words, use the word-based technique below. If you are more deeply moved by images, go with the imagery-based technique. If you cannot decide which will serve you more powerfully, do both. You can also do a combined version in which you add illustrations to words and words to your picture.

(*Hint:* If you do both, you are better prepared for whatever curve balls come your way!)

Word-based technique:

- Write a letter (or a song or a poem!) to your future self describing in detail how you feel right now. Talk about the reasons you want to make changes; describe how you currently feel about yourself, your body, your situation. Include any difficulties you are having because of your weight or lifestyle. Do not forget to include health concerns or fears about what the future may hold if your weight continues to increase. Then, describe the changes you want for which you are prepared to work. Be specific; talk about how you want to feel and what positive impact the changes may have on your life. Remind your future self how much this effort means to you today and how important it is even if at the moment your future self is reading this, you may be frustrated or tired. Read this letter every few weeks, and certainly whenever you feel your determination slipping.

Imagery-based technique:

- Draw or create a collage of images that express where you are now and where you want to go. Divide your picture surface into two halves with one side representing how you currently feel, and the other showing what you want to achieve. Don't be shy—create a detailed, vibrant expression of what is driving you to begin this journey and what pleasing abilities, events, and outcomes you anticipate as it progresses. I *do not* suggest you post this picture where you will see it every day. Doing so will eventually make it invisible as you get so used to seeing it that you no longer really *see* it. A better strategy is to keep it in a safe place and, as you do with the letter to your future self, look at it every few weeks and when you need an extra reminder of what you are working toward.

Action Item

If right now is not a good time to write to your future self or create that image to ***bottle your motivational wind***, make a note on your calendar to do so on a specific day and time that does work. If you are planning to collage, begin collecting pictures (from magazines, the internet, etc.) over the next few days until your planned date. If you will be writing a letter, add a Wind memo to your smartphone in which you make note of ideas as they come to mind.

On the day at the time you planned to take this action, do so!

PLAN FOR THE UNPLANNED

If life were linear, we could be prepared for pretty much everything it throws at us. We would seldom, if ever, be caught without solutions for obstacles or find ourselves reacting before thinking. Happily, life is not linear. If it were, we would also be bored to tears and a million useful inventions would never have seen the light of day. So, enjoy the stimulation of our unpredictable existence, and plan for the unplanned.

What are landmines?

Landmines are those unexpected circumstances that blow up and derail you. Even if you have tried to manage your weight a hundred times in the past and already know that holiday feasts or lonely evenings are overeating triggers for you, I guarantee other landmines await that you don't expect. They are buried in the muck of things we tend not to think about.

Most people think it best to list the cons or negatives of remaining overweight and the pros or positives of losing weight. They believe that focusing on how lousy they feel now and how good they expect to feel later is enough to feed their motivation until they hit their target. They also think that being at that weight will keep them living happily ever after. Unfortunately, they are wrong.

This focus on pros of weight loss and cons of being overweight is to an extent what you have done while thinking through your motivations for weight change. We are going to expand your perspective now to examine the flip side of the coin.

There are many different reasons that people have difficulty achieving long-term weight objectives. In my experience, however, there is one reason that affects almost everybody, and that is failure to do a thorough analysis of the pros and cons of both *losing weight* and of *not losing weight*. They do not identify those aspects of their current lifestyle and their current weight that they really do not want to give up, and they fail to consider what they might not like about life at a lower weight.

People especially tend to overlook potentially scary aspects of weight loss. I remember one patient who dieted and regained the same excess pounds her entire adult life. It was not until she had been referred to me for weight regain after bariatric surgery that we figured out what was going on; when she lost weight, she looked more like her abusive mother. Irrational as it may have been, she unconsciously hated looking like her awful mother and so looking slimmer made her feel terrible. Having identified this landmine, my patient was able to address her fears rationally and ultimately achieve her goals.

Not all landmines are deep-seated like that of the patient I just described, but all are unnoticed triggers waiting to derail your plans and undermine your motivation.

NOTE: Bariatric surgery changes the configuration of the stomach and/or intestinal tract to make it uncomfortable to overeat, as well as in some cases make the body absorb less of what you eat.

How do I find my landmines?

Step 1: Create a Weight Loss Resume of several of your most recent weight management attempts. As you would for an employment resume, begin with your most recent effort and record start/end dates, how much weight you lost and how long you kept how much of it off. For each effort, also list key strategies used (e.g., low-carb menu, food records, group meetings, etc.), and how difficult or easy they were to stick with as well as how useful each one felt. Review the results to determine whether there are any particular strategies that work well for you—those that you were able to follow most easily and those that produced the best results. Also identify those that blew up on you time and again— they were great on paper but simply did not fit your personality or life circumstances. This first level of your landmine map lets you know what approaches to definitely avoid and which *possibly* to incorporate as you go forward. Finally, look at the resume through the eyes of someone who does not know you and does not know your weight history. Look for your strengths—how many times you have tried despite disappointment, how many difficult or odd strategies you have valiantly grappled with, what obstacles have you powered through despite difficulty? You have a lot more going for you than you think!

Here is what Camila's Weight Loss Resume looked like.

Start/ End	Pounds Lost	Regained over time	Key Strategies & Effectiveness/ Difficulties
7 wks. this year	8	10 lbs., 8 wk.	Ketogenic. Got harder each week, ultimately made me miserable.
Last year, approx. 12 wks.	15	19 lbs., 5 mo.	Detailed menu from a commercial program, 3 meals and 2 snacks each day. Not too hard to follow except I really missed my favorite foods and each time I broke the diet for one of them, my commitment flagged. By the end of the three months, I was barely following the plan at all and feeling pretty hopeless.
Last year, about 3 wks.	5	8 lbs., 1 mo.	Food combinations to match my blood type. I've since learned that this is nonsense. However, it helped in that I was so nervous about eating the 'wrong' foods, that I mostly avoided eating when I could. Till I got really, really hungry and gave up.
2 yrs. ago, about 4 mos.	20	27 lbs., 6 mo.	Kept calories to about 1800/day. Not too difficult as I could eat anything I wanted as long as I hit my target. I ran into trouble during the holidays and the party foods made the target harder to hit. With each over-target day, it became harder to refocus until I decided that I'd blown it and would restart on New Year day. That didn't happen.

Camila's Conclusion:

Obviously, following other people's menu plans doesn't work for me. I either miss 'my' foods too much or get overwhelmed with the rules. Calorie-counting was the most effective for me although I clearly didn't handle missed targets very well. Going forward, I will focus on developing the habits that make it easier for me to enjoy my preferred foods but in reasonable quantities. Also, I really need to rethink my approach to slips. Just imagine—if two years ago I had handled the holiday feasting differently and maybe stopped losing weight during December but not regained (or not regained more than a couple pounds), I'd be in an entirely different place right now!

Action Item

Build your **Weight Loss Resume**. If you have difficulty remembering the details of each past effort, get the resume started and then come back to it in a few hours or tomorrow. You will most likely find that once you start thinking about this, memories come back to you.

Step 2: Create a Pros/Cons Matrix of the advantages and disadvantages of losing weight and of not losing weight. As you complete your matrix, think outside the usual box of health impact and appearance. For instance, think about what cutting back on eating out might do to your social life, or what activities you might have to skip to make time for meal-prep or exercise. Also give thought to the possible emotional benefits of not losing weight such as a sense of protection from unwanted romantic/sexual advances, pay-back at a family member who has made you feel bad about your weight, or something to blame for life disappointments. The more honest you are with yourself about the benefits of staying as you are, and the anxieties related to losing weight, the more likely you are not to trip on them as you move forward.

Here is what Marta's Pros/Cons Matrix looked like.

	Pros	Cons
Living at a Lower Weight	Improved health Get off some of my meds Look better Easier to move around More confidence Make spouse happy Easier to buy clothing	Have to give up favorite foods Takes a lot of work Uncomfortable attention from others Might find out life's problems are not all because of my weight Live with fear of regain Higher expectations of me by others
Staying at Current Weight	Don't have to give up favorite foods No pressure to exercise Don't have to think about stuff Just easier Won't be disappointed when I regain	Worsening health Keep getting heavier Hard to participate in life Feel ugly Tire easily Spouse losing interest Feeling overlooked by others

Action Item

Start your ***Pros/Cons Matrix*** right now. Set up two columns intersected by two rows. Label the columns *Pros* and *Cons* and label the rows *Living at a Lower Weight* and *Staying at Current Weight*. Then start filling in the squares. In addition to the obvious appearance and health aspects of weight, reflect on the less commonly discussed impacts weight has on an individual in our society, in your family, and so on.

As you move forward, return to this matrix periodically to remind yourself of where you began, as well as update it as you make new discoveries about yourself and your relationship to your body.

How do I avoid my landmines?

Having identified several landmines, you are in a good position to avoid tripping on them. Problem-solve, plan ahead, and mentally rehearse how you will handle each one if it occurs. If any of them are so emotionally loaded that you cannot see yourself successfully managing them on your own, seek help from a trusted friend or a therapist.

One more thing to keep in mind about landmines. Most are not completely avoidable. However, the more you are aware and the more you prepare, the less damage they do. When you do hit a landmine, remember that you can use that experience to strengthen your skillset and make it less likely that you have the same problem down the road.

Surely health concerns will keep me motivated!?

Yes, to an extent. If you have recently experienced a serious health scare, odds are you are very motivated to follow doctor's orders and take care of your body. Similarly, if you have recently had an 'aha' experience about the risk you face, motivation will be strong. As time goes by, however, the hard work of changing lifelong patterns will start to weigh on you and it will become easier and easier to put off the effort for tomorrow, or next Monday.

How do I use health as a motivator?

That is the million-dollar question. The medical world has spent the last century advertising the risks of unhealthy behaviors in an effort to motivate people to make health-enhancing changes. They have not been terribly effective.

In my experience, one key to making health a stable motivator is linking it to more immediate and tangible desires. For instance, the exercise routine that promotes intangible cardiovascular health also tangibly improves your stamina for mowing your lawn or playing tag with your kids. Similarly, enhancing your nutritional intake lowers your cholesterol (intangible) and improves your digestion (tangible).

Another key to using your health as a motivator is to use self-talk to link health-promoting behaviors to personal values. For instance, telling yourself, "Taking care of my health protects my autonomy by keeping me strong enough to take care of myself as I age," or "Being a good role model for others depends on my own self-care."

Won't my shrinking body motivate me?

Yes and no. The thought of losing weight and looking more like your beauty ideal can certainly be motivating. However, for reasons described in the next answer, body changes seldom create the motivational magic we expect. What they often do create, unfortunately, is motivational death as your body does not change as quickly and as noticeably as you hope.

Why not rely on my shrinking body for motivation?

There are three reasons that relying exclusively on your body for motivation is not a great idea. First of all, the body areas you are most focused on are not necessarily going to be the ones that change most quickly or early in the process. Thus, you may be gradually and consistently losing evenly across your body but not seeing loss in the area you feel most self-conscious; and therein lies discouragement and a sucker punch to your motivation.

The second reason your body can be a poor motivator is that our perception of body size tends to change more slowly than our actual body does. Any woman who has ever been pregnant can vouch for that as she discovered (sometimes by means of a painful run-in with furniture edges) that how far she perceived her stomach to protrude often lagged behind how quickly it grew. Similarly, patients who rapidly lose massive amounts of weight with bariatric surgery or fasts, often complain that despite the numbers on the scale, they see themselves just as heavy as before the procedure.

The third thing that makes it tricky to rely on body changes is that our body perception, our body image, is a complicated piece of work. It is based in part on our physical reality and in part on how we feel about and evaluate that physical reality. Indeed, a rich body of research (pun totally intended) has established that body image dissatisfaction can easily be triggered by manipulating to whom people compare themselves or what sort of appearance feedback they receive. Hence, you might be bopping along feeling quite good about the impact of your efforts and then run into an old 'friend' who looks fantastic and makes unkind references to your size—bam! You go from feeling optimistic and motivated to what's-the-use sad. So, relying on your body perception to keep you focused on your goals … not such a great plan.

How do I improve my body image?

There is a two-pronged answer to this question. One entails using physical markers to challenge body misperceptions, and the other is expanding your body image. (Do not panic! I said expand your body *image*, not your body!)

Physical markers are simply concrete things that illustrate body changes. Here are a few:

- Save a pre-weight-loss pair of trousers and shirt/blouse. After every several pounds decrease, try on the outfit and measure how many centimeters of extra space exists between the fabric and you. Keep a dated record of the results.

- Record your weight on a graph every week. Expect there to be weeks during which the scale does not move at all and weeks it does. Evaluate your progress by looking at your trajectory over four weeks—if the trend line is gently moving down, you are doing fine. If it is not moving down, you will need to tweak your approach.

- Keep a monthly record of your waist measurement. (Measure your waist by placing a tape measure just above your bellybutton, keeping the tape horizontal, and pulling it snug but not so snug that it compresses your skin.) Do not expect your waist to decrease nearly as quickly as your weight. In general, waist size will not decrease an inch until more than eight pounds are lost; and keep in mind this is a general average that describes a generic person. Your experience will be unique to you and may well fluctuate over time.

NOTE: If you are doing a lot of muscle-building exercise while you reduce your weight, you may find that your waist loses inches before the scale registers weight loss. This means you are likely losing adipose (fat) while adding muscle which is heavier than adipose.

Action Item

Set up two spreadsheet *graphs* or use plain old-fashioned graph paper to record today's date and your current *weight* on one and the date and your *waist measurement* on the other. Mark each graph with the next measurement date and save them in a safe place. Place a reminder in your calendar to ensure you reweigh next week, and remeasure next month.

Expand your body image by broadening your focus from weight and appearance to include function. Folks who struggle with overweight tend to let the size of their bodies blind them to other wonderful aspects of their physical state. They forget it is their body that allows them to experience the joy of music or read a thrilling book (or this book!). They ignore the fact that it is their amazing eyes and hands that create art or quickly prevent their toddler or cat from knocking over a houseplant. Think about the people you love and the things you love to do, and think about all the body parts (skin, eyes, nerves, muscles, etc.) that allow those experiences.

Camila

Remember Camila, the single mom who discovered that planning and preparing meals actually ate up less time than waiting in fast-food drive-through lines? That was not the only epiphany she had.

As she became more at ease with me, she slowly dropped her initial stance that her only reason for seeking help to reduce her weight was to "be healthy for my kids." While being around for her kids was certainly important to her, Camila soon admitted that what was really driving her motivation was how much she hated her body. This was problematic for two reasons. The obvious one was that all that hating was exhausting and hard to deal with. The less obvious one was that she, unintentionally, also used that hatred as an excuse to stop trying—the (distorted) reasoning behind this was that she/her body was so ugly that she/it did not deserve to be well-cared for. I know, illogical but not unusual.

Camila and I spent much of that session talking about all the body aspects, other than appearance, to which she typically paid no attention. We talked about how much she loved the children her body had created, the physical joy of soaking in a hot bath, the wonderful sensations of good food, massage, hiking in the mountains, reading books, … No doubt in part to get me to back off, Camila did agree by session's end that she would give more thought to this and write a thank-you letter to her body before our next session. She did.

Over the next few weeks, Camila noticed a shift in her thinking. When she mis-managed a high-risk situation or flat-out decided to overeat, those incidents began to lose their power to make her feel like a failure. She could give herself permission to deviate from her plan confident that she still knew how, and deserved, to take care of her wonderful body/self.

Action item

Write a *letter of apology and thanks to your body*. Write the letter from the perspective of imagining your body is a friend of yours whom you have failed to appreciate and periodically mistreated over the years. Talk about the joys it has allowed you throughout your life. Also talk about the nasty things you have said (thought) about it. Apologize for the torture you have inflicted in the way of restrictive diets and grueling workout routines. Tell it that you appreciate its work on your behalf regardless of its weight and what you plan to do to make amends and treat it better going forward. Save this letter for when you need to be reminded.

NOTE: If negative body image consistently gets in the way of you enjoying life, consider the possibility of an eating disorder (see Do I have an eating disorder?) and engaging with a therapist. If you do not feel the problem is sufficiently significant to require therapy, consider purchasing my favorite book on the subject, The Body Image Workbook: An Eight-Step Program for Learning to Like Your Looks, by Dr. Thomas Cash.

How should I reward myself for weight loss?

Do not. Weight loss is not something you *do* so there is no reason to reward yourself for it. There are *things you do that cause weight loss,* so it makes more sense to reward yourself for those actions. Completing all or most Action Items in a chapter, or consistently practicing a new behavior for a period of time are reward-worthy items.

In terms of what constitutes a reward, the most powerful reward you can use is self-talk that is opposite to that you have used in the past to berate yourself for your overweight and the behavior that fed it. In place of negative thoughts about yourself, intentionally focus on telling yourself that you are doing the work of making change, that you have consistently done [this or that behavior] and that is proof that you are moving forward.

Help yourself develop rewarding self-talk by periodically updating your *Pros/Cons Matrix* to flesh out your items describing the pros of living at a lower weight. As you integrate the recommended behaviors into your lifestyle, pay attention to the sense of mastery that emerges and add those positive feelings to the Matrix. Working on this will gradually rescript your inner monologue and the result will be more rewarding than even the most expensive gift you could buy.

MOVING WITHOUT MOTIVATION

Despite your best efforts, there will be times you are simply not feeling it. You will review your motivating reasons, your letters and images and matrices and lists—and just not want to take the next step, literally or figuratively. Most people at this point quit. What they do not know is that motivation and action are reciprocal forces. Life is easiest when motivation drives our behavior. However, when the behavior is goal-directed, the act of doing can also drive motivation. Hence, your job at times like this is to keep doing what you need to do.

This is when you need to get creative. Whether you do that by changing your self-talk, reaching out to others, or overhauling your environment is entirely dependent on your personality, your life situation, and the particular moment in time you need the push. In other words, different strokes for different folks and different strokes at different times. (Sorry, I could not resist the old song reference.)

What self-talk helps?

The best self-talk is that which is personally meaningful. Given I do not know you personally, I cannot tell you what words will ring true for you. You need to figure it out for yourself but here are suggestions to get you thinking:

- The reasons this was important to me yesterday (or last week or …) are still important even though I'm not feeling it right now. If I quit now, I'll be really sad tomorrow.
- I do not have to feel it to do it.
- Life cannot always be smooth, and this is one of those time I need to muscle through.
- Sucks to be me right now. (Note: The implication is that this rough patch is temporary.)
- I can feel lousy and do what I need to do anyhow.
- The only thing that's changed since I decided I need this is my mood and I will not let moods run my life!
- So my motivation has gone underground. That just means I need to work around it for now.

What self-talk hurts?

The most damaging self-talk falls into two categories.

1. *Mis-labeling of action.* This happens when you slip up in your self-management plans, conclude you are no longer 'doing it,' (over-generalization), and label the action as something you no longer do. For example, missing a workout (or a week of workouts) is framed as no longer exercising instead of having not exercised today or this week or … There is a critical difference between "I used to exercise" and "I didn't exercise today (or this week)."

2. *Mis-labeling of worth.* Also triggered by a lapse in plan adherence, this refers to the conclusion that you are not worthy of the desired goals because you erred. Mis-labeling of worth is an example of emotional reasoning;

you conclude you are bad and unworthy because you feel so bad about the error. For example, "I really messed up my exercise routine. I suck. I'm just not worth the effort." A more helpful response to the missed workouts would be, "I messed it up but gotta give myself credit for trying. I'll figure out what went wrong and take the next right step."

Be on the lookout for mis-labeling of action. Now that you are aware of it, you should have a relatively easy time catching yourself and correcting the self-talk. When you catch yourself mis-labeling your worth, use the corrective self-talk guidance provided in the Foundation chapter.

How do I manage weight plateaus?

If you have more than a few pounds to lose, you are going to hit weight loss plateaus. This is your body's natural response to the combined impact of carrying less weight and the metabolic slowdown caused by caloric restriction. You can look at plateaus as obstacles to your progress, *or* you can look at them of evidence of your progress. The plateau means that you have changed your body composition enough to have an impact. In other words, what you are doing is working! If you stay with your plan, giving your body a chance to settle into its rhythm, you will resume losing weight in a few weeks or months.

If you are logging your food and exercise and are sure that you are following your plan fairly consistently, but weight loss does not restart within a month or so, there are few steps you can take:

- Increase your physical activity. If you do so, be sure to do it in a fashion that you are able to sustain. Do not go overboard. Increase your time or intensity or frequency a small amount at a time. If you jump ahead too far, you are likely to be too miserable to repeat it. On the other hand, if you increase slowly, you can comfortably add more if needed.

- The other option for activity adjustment is to change the exercise you are doing. When we do the same routine for extended periods of time, our muscles become efficient with those movements and so the caloric cost decreases. Switching to a new routine might up the calorie cost of your workout just enough to push your weight off the plateau.

- Decreasing your caloric intake is also an option although it risks further slowing your metabolism and extending the plateau. If you do go this route, decrease your intake in small degrees. Large decreases will likely result in a quick weight drop and then rapid regain as your metabolism is further depressed.

- If you give it your best effort and the plateau seems to be ongoing, adopt the plateau weight as your current goal and *practice maintaining it.* The truth of the matter is that you will not be losing weight forever and at some point you will have to get comfortable maintaining your weight. The more practice you have earlier in the process, the better the long-term outlook. Moreover, if you are nowhere near your targeted healthy range, after a few months of maintenance, you may find that it becomes easy to resume weight loss with minor changes to your daily behavior.

- Finally, consider the possibility that this weight is the one that your genetics and lifestyle can sustain. If that is the case, ask yourself if you would prefer to weigh what you did before starting this journey, or whether you would prefer to live at your current weight. My guess is that your new, lower weight is preferable—so defend it!

Should I ask others for support?

Many people find it helpful to have an external support person when they are making difficult changes. Even if you are working with a therapist, it is helpful to have someone in your personal circle who knows you well enough to offer encouragement without irritation. You can set this up by telling that person or those people what you are doing and ask them to check in with you periodically, or simply ask them to be on stand-by for a pep talk when you tell them you need it. How you structure this depends entirely on your personality and the nature of your relationships.

Is the buddy system a good idea?

Embarking on weight management with a buddy can be wonderfully helpful. It can also be stupendously unhelpful. Unfortunately, I have no information about you and your potential buddy on which to base a recommendation. I can, however, encourage you to consider a few things before committing:

- Are you comfortable receiving feedback from others, or does feedback more often than not feel like criticism?

- Is the buddy you are considering someone who knows

how to frame feedback constructively, or does his or her help often feel like a slap?

- Are you and the buddy contemplating similar approaches to your goals? If you are, that may be helpful as the two of you problem-solve similar challenges. On the other hand, if either of you tends to get competitive, the similarity in your strategies and goals could become toxic.

- How much of your motivation stems from the idea of doing this together versus from the idea of doing this regardless of whether anyone else is involved?

- What is your fallback strategy if your buddy bails?

How can environment help?

In addition to the stimulus control strategies outlined in the Environment & Hunger chapter, it may help to restructure you temporal and physical environment to get you through the rough patch.

In terms of temporal restructuring, brainstorm ways to re-arrange your schedule to make it easier for you to complete the tasks that move you toward your goals. For instance, if hitting your daily step target is the challenge, you might shift your schedule to allow you to move more in the morning before the day wears you down. Or if fixing healthy dinners on work nights starts to feel more like work than self-care, shift the bulk of your meal preparation to the weekend and use that marvelous invention, the microwave, to quickly warm up those dinners.

Potentially helpful changes to your physical environment range from setting up a whiteboard of daily to-do items that you check off (or give yourself gold stars for—whatever rings your bell), to setting an alarm to remind you to stand up and move every so often, to storing your stinky gym bag in the car so you have no excuse to go home and end up changing into pajamas rather than working out.

Obviously, the examples I provide are generic. You will need to figure out what obstacles are making it difficult for you at this time and how to work around them. If you keep pushing forward, motivation will resurface.

Action Item

Given we cannot predict when or why you will run out of motivational steam, the best way to prepare for those times is to create a motivational equivalent of the cellphone contact ICE (In Case of Emergency) which tells emergency personnel who you are and who to contact when you are unable to speak for yourself. Your *Motivational ICE* can be a card (paper or electronic) you keep with you that lists ideas, including corrective self-talk, to keep you moving forward—or minimally not sliding backward—until you once again feel inspired.

MOTIVATION ROUNDUP

Motivation is a slippery thing. It is not something you 'get' like a new house that you proceed to live in for 20 years. The 'getting' of it is more like getting an energy burst. It pushes you forward for a while until you tire and then you need to push yourself to take the next steps and appropriate actions to replenish your energy reserves. For physical energy, these steps would entail rest and nourishment. For motivation, these steps are the work you have begun in this chapter. Taking care of your motivation must begin today (yesterday would be even better) and continue into the future.

Make the time now to really think about what it is you hope to accomplish and why. As you do so, emphasize what it is about your objectives that is truly about you and not others; the most powerful motivators are those that are personally meaningful. Think it through carefully and make those thoughts reality by writing them, illustrating them, composing a song about them … anything to make them tangible! From there, invest energy in figuring out what has knocked you off course in the past. You cannot avoid something you cannot see and identifying your landmines is the way to see them. Exploring past weight management efforts not only helps you map landmines, it also helps you identify your strengths.

Finally, think about your body. Your wonderful, hard-working, forgiving body. No matter how many times and in how many ways you have mis-treated it with crazy weight loss schemes, here it is. Holding you up, taking you places, empowering you to love, laugh, live! It is for this unfailingly loyal 'friend,' that you are making the time and investing the energy to enhance your lifestyle.

Action Step Recap:

1. ***Record every reason in your motivational bag.*** Clearly state what you want to work toward and *why* that goal is important to you.

2. ***Bottle today's motivation*** by writing a letter to your future self or creating artwork that describes in detail what is fueling your motivation—how you are feeling now and how you expect and hope to feel if you persevere.

3. Create a **Weight Loss Resume** to figure out what strategies have been easiest for you to use in the past and what dead-ends you want to avoid revisiting.

4. Complete a **Pros/Cons Matrix** to identify all the obvious forces that are pulling you toward weight management (i.e., the pros of weight loss and cons of not losing weight) and the hidden forces (i.e., the cons of weight loss and pros of not losing weight) that may get in your way.

5. **Begin graphing** your weight weekly, and your waistline monthly.

6. **Write an apology and thank you letter** to your body. Acknowledge its wonderful care of you.

7. Think ahead to the times that you will not feel motivated and create a **Motivational ICE** plan to help you keep moving.

MAINTENANCE MINDER

If you have already completed your *Personal Weight Profile* to set a reasonable weight-range goal and begun a Log to track your intake and challenges, you are well-begun. Pat yourself on the back. If you have not done so, now is a good time.

Continue to pay attention to your self-talk, noting the *cognitive distortions* that trigger you to make poor decisions and scripting *rational rebuttals* to minimize their impact. Also, take note of your high-risk situations and use *CPR* to plan ahead for how best to manage them.

If you have not yet done *The Stomach Exercise*, do yourself a favor and get on it! As you move forward, you will find that having taken the time to identify your body's hunger and satiety signals will make your journey much easier.

MOTIVATION FOR PARENTS

For the most part, your motivational struggles are not something that should be shared with your children. Children who grow up hearing their parents denigrate their own bodies or abilities tend to grow up to do the same. Even if you think that your child will learn to take better care of his or her body by seeing how you struggle to care for yours, I can almost guarantee this will backfire. Most likely, the child will develop the same negative body image that you have, or become so obsessed with food and exercise control that she or he develops a mental disorder (e.g., eating disorders, body dysmorphic disorder, obsessive-compulsive disorder).

What I do encourage you to share with your children is why you make healthy choices, and model how you actively cope with frustration and occasional lack of motivation. For example, you can comment aloud on how lucky we are that fruit and vegetables that help us grow and stay healthy are also so delicious, or how taking a walk after school or work refreshes us. Reflect aloud how you are going to do some task or chore that you are not in the mood to do simply because it is important, and how good it feels to get the job done. When you are frustrated, 'think' out loud as you calm yourself and problem-solve. For instance, "Gritting my teeth (or cussing or throwing things …) is not going to help me solve this so I will take a moment to breathe and think of a better solution."

Modeling effective coping skills is one of the great gifts we can give our children.

CHAPTER 5

ENVIRONMENT & HUNGER

No one lives in a vacuum. From womb to tomb, we interact with our environment. Before birth, our environment is mom's body. Then, birth brings a dramatic expansion to our environment. It becomes the people with whom we interact, the physical spaces we occupy, and the information to which we are exposed. From all this interaction, we learn about our world and ourselves, and we are shaped by what we learn. That shaping is sometimes obvious as in who teaches us what, but oftentimes it is not obvious. Not-obvious shaping is that subtle pairing of events such as love and food that leaves us 'feeling loved' when we eat certain foods or sad when access to them is denied.

Right now, I am resisting the urge to write 10,000 pages dazzling you with everything I have learned about learning. How humans make connections between events, and between themselves and those events is complex and fascinating. Nonetheless, I suspect if it tickled you as much as it does me, you would already have taken those classes. So I shall desist. Instead, here is the short version.

Every time we interact with our environment, a connection is made. For instance, each time you eat in front of the television, your brain links the television to eating. When you look at a slice of pizza, pick it up, and experience the yum, the power of pizza to trigger eating grows regardless of hunger. Similarly, when you are sad and a steaming cup of cocoa distracts you from your sadness, the act of drinking cocoa (or hot liquids or sweetness) is linked to feeling better. (All those break-up movies in which the heart-broken partners curl up with tubs of ice-cream are prime examples of this!)

Defining environment is more complex than first meets the eye. Obviously, the physical space in which you operate is 'environment.' However, the people with whom you interact also are 'environment,' as are the physical sensations of your body and your emotions. Almost everything we do in terms of managing emotions, hunger, and exercise modifies aspects of our environment and how it affects us.

Despite the intricately interwoven nature of all components of our environment, I have roughly organized this chapter into those aspects pertaining to your physical environment, and those pertaining to your social environment. However, as you proceed, keep in mind that boundaries between physical and social (and emotional) are artificial and your experience will seldom feel like it neatly fits into one category or the other.

PHYSICAL ENVIRONMENT

Included in our discussion of the physical environment is why you react to it the way you do, and how to decrease its power over you and move your reactions in a healthier direction.

Why is food on my mind more than it is for my thin friends?

The jury is still out on whether genetic differences or experience (learning history) account for the greater portion of what determines your sensitivity to food cues. We are sure of only two things. One is that some combination of genetics and experience determines your sensitivity to and preoccupation with food. The other thing we know is that people with chronic overeating are in fact more sensitive to environmental and emotional eating triggers than those who do not struggle to moderate their intake[6,7,8,9].

In simple terms, you probably experience the sight, smell, and thought of favorite foods as more appealing than your non-overweight friends. Moreover, it is also possible that bite for bite, you receive more pleasure from your food than do people who do not struggle with overeating. In other words, environmental eating triggers have a bigger impact when they hit you than when they hit your chronically thin friends.

Will I forever be a slave to my environment?

Yes and no.

Yes, your behavior is always and forever entangled with your environment—you do not and cannot exist in a vacuum.

No, the relationship between you and your environment need not be one in which you are the slave. To the contrary, you can take control and arrange your environment to lessen its negative impact and increase its positive impact.

How do I master my physical environment?

There are simple environmental changes you can make to help you more easily manage your weight. However, be forewarned! Although the changes are simple, making them requires serious effort.

All the techniques stem from the fact that our minds automatically link setting, behavior, and outcome. The result is that if in a given setting you repeatedly do something that feels good, that setting will come to make you want to do that behavior whether or not doing it makes sense at the time. For instance, imagine that you are in the habit of coming home from work, taking your dinner into the TV room, kicking back on the sofa, clicking on the remote, and eating dinner while watching TV. Do that often enough and eventually even if you go out for a big dinner after work and arrive home thoroughly stuffed, when you settle in front of the TV, the first thing that pops into your head is, "Hmmm… might want something to eat."

Managing your eating behavior starts with limiting the number of unhelpful places, things, and activities that stimulate you to overeat. We call these strategies *stimulus control*. Some strategies are easier and some more difficult to implement. None, however, require more energy investment than some of the zanier diets you have tried in the past!

What is the easiest change to make?

Structure your space—and by 'structure,' I mean get rid of those foods that are typically hard for you not to over-indulge. If a bowl of M&Ms on your desk continuously screams your name, for heaven's sake, fill the bowl with marbles, or replace the bowl with a plant or picture—or simply clear your desk!

Action Item

Structure your space. Review your Log and survey your home and workspaces for foods that repeatedly make you eat or overeat regardless of hunger and give them away or toss them in the trash. Then stop buying them. You do not need to keep these high-risk foods in your living spaces.

However, do not promise yourself never to eat these foods again. You enjoy them and deserve to enjoy them— but enjoy them elsewhere, in places you do not spend so very much of your time.

How do I defuse high-risk foods?

There are always likely to be foods in your home or workspace that are especially hard for you to not overeat. In fact, just about any desirable food can become a high-risk item if it is readily accessible. Reducing the power of these foods to derail your self-care plans can be done with the following strategies:

- *Store all food out of sight.* Keep it in the kitchen inside the pantry or fridge. If it is not visible, you will not be forced to think about it every time you turn around.

- *Store packaged high-risk food (i.e., those foods that are hard to resist when you are reminded of them) in opaque (not transparent) wrappers or containers.* This decreases their visual impact and requires you to do extra work to eat them. While the extra step of opening a storage container is not necessarily a deterrent, it does give you that extra moment to consider your choice before facing photo-shopped images of perfect foods that are hard to resist.

- *Make accessing high-risk foods require more effort* than healthier options. In the fridge, freezer, and pantry place them toward the back of the shelf; preferably behind something taller and wider and healthier.

- ***Do not make any food strictly off limits.*** Completely swearing off a favorite food is a good way to make it irresistible. Think about it. If this is something you really enjoy and you decide you will resist it forever, you have to invest energy and attention into not eating it. In other words, you need to think about it. A lot. Foods that are tricky and tempting are best assigned to the sometimes category, and either bought in single servings you bring home for a treat or enjoyed somewhere you have to make an effort to visit.

Action item

Defuse high-risk foods. Walk through your home and move any food items that are in the living room or bedrooms into the kitchen pantry or fridge. Survey your fridge, freezer, and pantry for high-risk items and do two things: (1) place them in opaque containers, and (2) move them to the back of the shelf, behind healthier options.

If you have promised yourself to never again, or until you weigh your imagined perfect number, eat a particular food, promise yourself to never again make that promise. In its place, develop a strategy for when and where you will enjoy that item.

The entire world makes me overeat!

Not really a question but I get the point. Having spent a lifetime eating at the table, on the sofa, in the car, at your desk, in bed, at work, on the balcony, at the movies, …, all those places have become eating cues. The only way to lessen their trigger power is by means of a psychological mechanism called *extinction*. This means you extinguish their power by intentionally not engaging in the behavior while they are present.

Well, that was a convoluted way of saying, "Do not eat in all those places!" Each time you sit on the sofa, go to the movies, get into bed, etc. without eating, those stimuli lose a little bit of their power. With enough practice, you will be able to be in those places without thinking about food, and if you do think of it, the urge will be more easily managed.

It is worth noting that when you first begin to limit the places in which you eat, you will feel uncomfortable. When that happens, as it inevitably will, you have two options. You can either escape the discomfort by eating in that location, or you can recognize that discomfort as a sign that you are making an important change. In other words, in this case discomfort is a good sign. Pat yourself on the back and take delight in knowing that you are moving toward your goals.

How do I extinguish the world?

Restrict eating to a single **Designated Eating Place (DEP)** at home and, as much as possible, at work or school. This will limit the number of environmental cues that are repeatedly associated with eating and make you want to eat whether or not you are hungry.

Your DEP will ideally be a place that can be used *only* for eating. I strongly recommend that you make the kitchen or dining-room table your DEP at home and the cafeteria or break-room the DEP at work or school. If your work or school does not have a space that would work as a DEP, create a temporary DEP by clearing your workspace and eating on a placemat which you put away after your meal. This changes the look of your workspace so that you are not linking it to eating/hunger, while the new place setting provides a new stimulus configuration to which eating is linked.

Action item

Decide what your *Designated Eating Place (DEP)* will be at home and at work or school. Commit to eating only at your DEP—regardless of whether you are eating a small snack or an enormous meal, the DEP is where you will be!

If your work or school setting does not have a physical place you can designate, buy a placemat and utensil set that can be easily rolled up and stashed in a backpack, purse, locker, or desk drawer. Use this to create a DEP when you must eat in that setting.

Why does everything I do make me want to eat?

As is the case for the places of your life, the activities that you link to eating take on their own stimulus power. If you often play videogames or read while eating, those activities will trigger desire for food. Any activity repeatedly paired with eating has taken on stimulus power that you must now begin to extinguish.

The stimulus control strategy that extinguishes the triggering power of activities is making the commitment to engage in no activities, other than conversation and/or listening to music, while eating. *No Simultaneous Activities* is one of the most difficult changes to make, especially if you live alone. Sitting by yourself at the table (DEP) with no one to talk to and nothing to watch or read can be uncomfortable. However, if you stick with it, you will find that not only does it get (a little) easier, but you will also discover that you are satisfied with less food than you thought possible. Engaging in no simultaneous activities makes it easier to pay attention to internal cues of hunger and satiety so you are more likely to feel 'done eating' before you feel stuffed.

Action Item

Review the reasons you want to manage your weight—both the good changes you anticipate and the negatives you want to escape. Then decide whether those objectives are worth a little discomfort right now. If they are and you have not already done so, decide on a *Designated Eating Place (DEP)* and commit to eating there and only there. Start with the very next bite you take!

When you have a week of DEP under your belt, further strengthen the power of this behavior by committing to *No Simultaneous Activities* while eating. If you share a home with others, ask them to stash their phones, turn off the television, leave their books elsewhere, and rediscover the pleasure of one another's company. If you live or eat alone, music or talk radio/podcasts are good company during your meal.

In your Log, add a location column and record DEP or wherever else you eat. If you do not stick to *No Simultaneous Activities* during an eating episode, be sure to record what you were doing while eating. This information will be useful as you move forward.

SOCIAL ENVIRONMENT

Managing your social environment is often key to managing your physical environment as you must negotiate compromises with people you live and/or work and study with. Doing so may cause discomfort as you change habitual ways of interacting, possibly triggering others to respond negatively and making you question your right to make changes. However, the changes are critical and you can accomplish them without dooming your social life. To do this requires the self-awareness that comes from identifying and challenging cognitive distortions that get in your way, and learning a handful of simple tricks to minimize your exposure to temptation while not depriving yourself of social pleasure.

What if my family needs my high-risk foods on hand?

Unless you live alone and work alone, accommodating other people's needs and preferences is simply a fact of life. If your relationships with those people allow you to ask for their support, by all means ask for their help in minimizing the presence of high-risk foods. If you are sure that is not an option in your situation, exert whatever power you do have to manage your exposure to those foods by using the strategies outlined in the next answer.

If you live with family members such as children for whom you are responsible, be careful not to confuse taking care of yourself with failing to care for them. It is not essential that you keep high-risk foods in your home "for the children" or your partner. The children will thrive just as well without BBQ potato chips or lasagna or whatever items are difficult for you. I promise you there will be no negative impact on your children's development if you primarily provide them with easy access to fruits and vegetables and whole grains and lean protein, and only moderate access to high-fat and high-sugar foods. In fact, given the genetic influence on bodyweight, your children will likely benefit from the change.

Juan's snacks

Once Juan got realistic about his weight goals, he had to figure out a way of eating that would move him toward a healthier weight but not require his entire family to change their lifestyle for him, as they had the three previous times he lost and regained weight. Given that his kids were all under 10 and growing like weeds, he wanted to be careful to neither interrupt their discovery of wonderful new foods, nor instill in them a fear of gaining weight. He and his wife spent some time considering the foods they usually kept in the home and identifying those that Juan's Log showed he most often over-consumed. It turned out that there really were only about three or four items that were particularly problematic: warehouse-sized jars of mixed nuts, regular sodas, graham crackers, and an assortment of salty chips. Juan and his wife then faced the task of deciding what to do about these.

Both Juan and his wife easily agreed the family could live quite well, indeed better, without sodas in the home and those got relegated to restaurant meals (about once per week). The graham crackers and chips were favorites of his children, so they made two changes. One was to alternate purchase of these so that both were not in the home simulta-neously, and the other was to buy them in smaller quantities so that if Juan overate, he would be edging out his children—something he did not want to do. The chips simply were relegated to occasional intake at parties elsewhere, and the decision was made to buy non-warehouse-sized jars of nuts and allow at least two weeks to elapse before replenishing when the container was empty.

With this strategy in hand, Juan's kids did not even notice the change and Juan did not feel like he was in a snack food desert. He also snacked a heck of a lot less.

NOTE: There is an important difference between fear of weight gain and desire to live at a healthy weight. Fear of weight gain carries the very real risk of triggering an eating disorder which, as I have said before, can kill you. Desire to live at a healthier weight means doing what is healthy for your body.

What self-talk makes it hard to manage social challenges?

There are two harmful self-talk (cognitive distortion) themes that most often occur in social settings when one is trying to moderate his or her intake. One is feeling self-conscious as you tell yourself others will notice your behavior and possibly 'judge' you. The other is feeling sorry for yourself because "it is not fair" that you have to pay attention to your intake.

What self-talk helps in social situations?

With respect to feeling self-conscious, the corrective self-talk is reminding yourself that the rest of the world is not nearly as interested in your behavior as you are. Hence, chances are that most people are not paying attention to what or how much you are eating. I know this is difficult to believe when you are feeling like the sore thumb, but I assure you it is true; most of us are occupied thinking about ourselves (and what others may be thinking of us)! As for those few individuals who may indeed be monitoring our behavior and passing judgement, here is your new self-talk for dealing with them:

- My choices are my business.

- I deserve to enjoy this event on my own terms.

- What and how much I eat is only my business.

- No one's happiness depends on me eating what they think I should.

- [*Name*] ought to get a life of their own and stop focusing on mine!

As for the self-pity party we may experience when stymied in our quest for complete gratification, remind yourself that you are the one who has *chosen* this path, and you have done so because it creates the life you desire. Hence, while others at the gathering are making choices that work for their lives, you are making choices that enhance your own. It helps also to think about the fact that social gatherings are, by definition, about people spending time together; food may be part of it, but is not the main course (sorry, I couldn't resist the pun). Helpful self-talk ideas:

- This will taste just as good in a smaller quantity.

- I'm here for the people. The food is just filler.

- This is not deprivation, this is self-care!

- The purpose of this event has nothing to do with what or how much I eat and everything to do with how much I enjoy my friends (colleagues, family).

- I am lucky that I have the freedom to carve my own path through social events.

Is it rude to refuse?

No. It is not rude to say no. You have the right to accept or reject food and drink (and other) offers if they are not to your liking or in your best interest.

That said, it is sometimes difficult to get others to back down when you tell them no. Here is a three-step strategy to help you elicit cooperation from others.

Step 1. Politely acknowledge, maybe even show appreciation for, the offer. This keeps the interaction friendly, no feelings are hurt, and the other person is neither put on the defensive nor triggered to go on the offense.

Step 2. Give your answer with an explanation to the extent that you feel it is that person's business. You can provide a rationale or keep it generic by simply stating you are not hungry, not in the mood right now, have other plans, etc.

Step 3. Thank the individual for honoring your request. Here is where we get a little sneaky because even if the person were about to hassle you about your choice, having already been graciously thanked for not doing so makes it harder not to honor your request.

To illustrate how this might sound, here is Louise's response to her supervisor's insistence that everyone have a piece of his birthday cake and then cornering Louise when he spotted her without a serving: "Jacques, you are so thoughtful, but I am still too full from lunch to be able to enjoy it without a bellyache. Thanks for not trying to tempt me!"

Can I eat out and lose weight?

Yes. Despite the fact that most American restaurants provide portions that are both larger and more calorically-dense than we tend to have at home, you can enjoy dining out without disrupting your self-care plans.

Ideally, you will moderate how often you eat out. Enjoying a larger meal now and then will not offset your efforts. Eating out multiple times per week, however, is likely to be counter-productive.

Regardless of how often you eat out, when selecting a restaurant it is helpful to preview their menu online to ensure they have offerings that fit your palate and your plan. If possible, opt for restaurants that serve you, rather than subject yourself to buffets and the many appealing items easily in reach.

What if I must eat out a lot?

Treat each restaurant as if it were your own kitchen. No, that does not mean nudge the chef aside and grab the spatula. It means tell the waiter what you want (e.g., with the side salad in place of fries) and how you want it prepared (e.g., grilled instead of fried). If the thought of doing this makes you uncomfortable, remember how much you are paying for this meal, compared to what it would cost to prepare at home (we are talking dollars to pennies here!). You are paying for the service. Make it work for you!

How do I eat out well?

Key to enjoying social meals without upsetting your self-care plans is accepting that enjoying these occasions is part of living in your healthy weight range. In other words, expect to have meals that stretch the boundaries of your self-care plans. Approach them as you would driving a manual-shift car when you have always driven an automatic. You would use all the knowledge and skill you have for driving in general, pay extra close attention to when you are changing gears, and not expect yourself to be perfect. When you dine out, have a general plan, be prepared to adjust as needed, and do not beat yourself up if it turns out differently than planned.

To minimize your exposure to overeating cues, consider the following tactics:

- If possible in the social setting, ask that the bread or chip basket not be placed on the table until the food arrives, or not be placed on the table at all. Having it before your entrée arrives and while you are still hungry makes it extremely difficult to avoid over-nibbling.

- Given that the average restaurant meal contains about half the number of calories an adult needs for an entire day[10], it helps to look at what the server brings you as providing not one, but two or possibly three meals. Before you dig in, use your knife to section off at least half of the serving and plan to take that extra portion home with you. You can ask for a to-go bag up front or at the end of the meal, whichever is easier for you. Another option is to order the appetizer version of that food as appetizers tend provide smaller portions.

- Focus on the conversation rather than the food and pace yourself so you are not the first to finish. If you eat slowly (see Mouth/Hand Rule in the next chapter), you will find yourself comfortably filling up well before running out of food.

- Do not look at the dessert options until you have finished your entrée and waited several minutes. Allowing your body to register the food it has received and recognize the lack of hunger will remove some the appeal from the desserts. If you do opt for dessert, consider sharing it with a friend.

ENVIRONMENT & HUNGER ROUNDUP

You are developing a clear picture of how powerfully linked your behavior is with the various contexts in which it occurs. These linkages are formed more quickly and more strongly between environment and eating than between environment and just about any other behavior. As a result, after a lifetime of eating all over the place while doing all manner of things, all those contexts have come to mean 'eat'.

Reducing the power of your environment to make you *over*eat requires that you rearrange things a bit. Storing food out of sight lessens how often you are triggered to think about it, and making it a little more difficult to grab slows impulse eating. Most powerfully, restricting intake to a *Designated Eating Place (DEP)* and not eating mindlessly by concurrently reading or watching a show, etc. will allow you to narrow the range of stimuli that make you feel hungry, and leave space for you to learn to listen to your body's actual signals for when it is time to eat and time to stop.

Managing the social aspects of your environment is anchored in your embrace of the fact that you have the right to ask for what you need and refuse that which you do not want. With that in mind, give yourself permission to enjoy social activities on your own terms. Do what you can to structure the social settings to help yourself (e.g., no breadbasket) and use your voice to politely assert your needs and take care of yourself.

There is one final point I want to emphasize before moving on. The objective of everything we discuss here is not to avoid eating. As I have said before, you must eat if you want to live (seems obvious but …)! The point is to *manage* your eating which means *mostly* eat in response to hunger and satiety and *sometimes* eat in response to other cues, *mostly* eat a comfortable amount of food and *sometimes* have to loosen your belt, and *mostly* make nutritious choices and *sometimes* eat something with almost no nutritional value but man oh man it tastes good! That, my friend, is happy healthy eating.

Action Step Recap:

1. **Structure your living space** to make it easier for you to make healthy food choices. Toss or donate high-risk foods you have in your home or work-space, and commit to enjoying them occasionally elsewhere. Stop bringing (most of) them home.

2. Given that it is neither reasonable, nor in many cases possible, not to have any tempting foods at home, make those items less visible and a little more work to get. **Defuse high-risk foods** by storing them in opaque containers and behind foods that present healthier options. Additionally, never keep food in any room of your home other than the kitchen.

3. Decide on a **Designated Eating Place (DEP)** at home and at work or school. If your work or school setting does not allow for a physically-distinct space in which to eat, prepare a portable placemat and table setting to keep with you and use when you must eat there.

4. Start eating only at your **DEP** and recording in your **Log** that you are doing so. Make a note about where you did eat when you deviate, and why.

5. When you have about one week of DEP under your belt, commit to **No Simultaneous Activities** while eating. That means you can talk with your meal-mates, enjoy music, talk radio, or a podcast, or simply savor the peace

and quiet and flavor of your meal—no reading, watching, or writing while you eat. Make a note in your Log when you deviate and why.

MAINTENANCE MINDER

If you are still reading and thinking about the things we have discussed, give yourself a hearty hurrah! As these ideas integrate with your current mindset and take root, you will find it easier to follow through on your weight management efforts.

Continuing to Log your intake and challenges is key to long-term success. As we discussed earlier, writing things down serves multiple purposes, and is especially important to habit change as it focuses your attention and helps consolidate memory. You can also use your Log to note changes you notice in your awareness of bodily hunger and satiety signals, as well as fluctuations in your mood as you navigate the highways and byways of behavior change. Having this information in a format you can truly 'see' will make it easier for to do the sort of problem-solving that would be possible if you were in therapy and had an objective observer giving you feedback.

Keep your motivation from fizzling out by reviewing and updating your Pros/Cons Matrix every few weeks. If your motivation lags, use the letter or graphic you developed to describe your goals to remind yourself that no matter how much of a pain it may be taking these steps, it was more painful living stuck in the hopeless mindset you had before you began.

I hope you are implementing (almost) all the Action Items recommended (most of the time). Each and every one has been carefully considered and selected from the proven techniques of the clinical world. However, if you are picking and choosing

Action Items, at a minimum complete the Pros/Cons Matrix, Motivational ICE Plan, and begin a weekly graph of your weight. Oh, and keep that Log going!

ENVIRONMENT & HUNGER FOR PARENTS

In reorganizing your home to keep food only in the kitchen and for the most part out of sight, you are making it much less likely that your children will develop the habit of eating in inappropriate places (e.g., bedroom) and at inappropriate times (e.g., while playing online). Further, as you make it a point to turn off screens, orchestrate family meals at your DEP (i.e., the table) and ban use of cellphones during meals, your children will also learn to disassociate eating with other places and activities. As your own healthy habits strengthen, so will those of your children.

I hope that by now you have come to understand the importance of flexibility in how you approach self-care. However, it is worth emphasizing how critically important that is in how you approach child-rearing. While it is reasonable to expect children to demonstrate increasing ability to adhere to family rules and expectations as they mature, it is also reasonable to expect parents to adjust their expectations and rules as children grow and their needs changes. As you implement my recommendations, be patient with yourself and with your children. It will take some back-and-forth movement until the whole family gets comfortable with the new structure, but it will happen if you keep pushing ahead. If you forget to do *No Simultaneous Activities* at breakfast, refocus for lunch and dinner. If your kids sneak snacks into the TV room, remind them of the rule and invite them into the kitchen to enjoy the snacks. Keep in mind that this is new for them as well.

CHAPTER 6

FOOD & HUNGER

Food fuels our lives. The substances we eat and drink are broken down by our body for its use. Without food, we die. Breathing air, drinking water, and eating food are the triple crown of no-brainer choices in life. Yet over the past half century, we have complicated food. Indeed, we have over-complicated it! Food has been cast in the role of villain as calories or carbs or fat or white food or food spelled with vowels and consonants have been trumpeted as the cause of obesity, early aging, fatigue—you name it. Alternatively, various foods have been heralded as the antidote to obesity, early aging, fatigue—you name it.

The result of all the casting and trumpeting has been a tremendous amount of publicized "information" about food. Where we used to go to the market and easily select foods we liked that were within our budget, we now become paralyzed in the grocery aisle as we waver between fat-free and wholly organic, between high-protein and low-fat or low-carb and high-fiber. It is enough to kill one's appetite! And it is *not necessary*.

In this chapter is the information you need to return to a simpler approach to food selection. The information is organized into three sections: *Basic* information about food, the relationship between food and your *Body*, and the *Behavior* that will help you manage your weight while enjoying your meals. The ultimate objective is to eat a variety of foods you enjoy and that meet your energy needs.

BASICS

While different cultures include and exclude different plants and animals from their diets, ultimately all humans require the same building blocks to stay alive. As you consider the material presented here, keep in mind that your body is not a machine. While all human bodies require the same basic building blocks, each individual body has its unique style of utilizing those building blocks to build health and wellness. As you gently shift your eating habits, track those changes in your Log and pay attention to how you feel. If you find yourself struggling to incorporate the nutrients you need, please consult a Registered Dietitian.

What is food?

Food, simply put, is anything we take into our bodies for nourishment. Whether in solid or liquid form, food is the group of substances that *literally* fuels our lives. Regardless of your culture and the specific plants and animals it considers food and non-food, all food eaten on our planet provides some combination of the nutrients without which our bodies cannot survive.

What is a calorie?

A calorie is a measure of energy. Scientifically speaking, a "calorie" is the amount of energy required to raise the temperature of one liter of water one degree centigrade at sea level. In useful words, the term "calorie" describes how much energy your body pulls from the food you eat.

"Calorie" is also a word that has come to have evil vibrations for both dieters and people with eating disorders. They see "calorie" as the enemy to be controlled and, if possible, avoided. That is a serious problem. Avoiding energy intake destroys you. You need to eat food to get energy to live. If you do not take in enough energy to fuel all your functions, your body cannibalizes itself. It breaks down fat to use the energy stored in it. Your body also breaks down muscle, including your heart, to fuel itself, and it stops repairing bone and other tissue as life wears away at it. Ultimately, if you do not eat enough food, you eat yourself.

So, strip the word "calorie" of its false meaning as the enemy of weight management, and think about it as an essential part of what you need to create a healthy body and stay alive to enjoy it.

Action item

If you need help making the transition from seeing calories as the enemy, *appreciate the work your body does* on an average day of living. It … : Generates 103,689 heart beats; Pushes blood to travel 168,000,000 miles (that's 168 *million*!); Takes 23,040 breaths; Inhales 428 cubic feet of air; Metabolizes 3.25 pounds of food; Processes 2.9 pounds of liquid; Sweats out 1.43 pints of liquid; Pushes out 7.8 pounds of waste (poop); Generates 85.6 degrees Fahrenheit of heat; Turns over 25 to 30 times during sleep; Moves 750 major muscles; Exercises 7,000,000 brain cells (that's 7 *million*!); Builds new cells to maintain hair, nails, skin, bones, teeth, blood, muscles, and all organs; Processes food into usable components; Calibrates body temperature and hydration levels to protect vital functions; Orchestrates

hormonal levels to promote and protect fertility.
Whew!

Is water food?

No. Water contains no calories and provides no nutrients. It is, however, essential to our health and survival. Without it, we die within a few days.

To tell whether you are drinking enough water, look at your urine. If it is dark and smelly, you are not sufficiently hydrated. A well-hydrated person produces urine that leans toward light yellow or clear and does not have a strong odor.

In addition to keeping you alive, proper hydration contributes to organ health and keeps your metabolism running smoothly. So, drink up!

What are macronutrients?

Macronutrients are the three major sources of fuel our bodies use. Pretty much all of the nutrients we need come from one of the three macronutrients: fat, carbohydrate, and protein.

Why do fat and sugar taste so good?

Because they are so important. Our taste buds know what we need! At least they knew what we needed before we become so adept at acquiring large amounts of food with extraordinarily little energy expenditure.

Fat and sugar taste good to us because they are calorically-dense foods that helped us survive in our native environments. Those of our ancestors who preferred these calorically-dense foods were able to take in enough energy to provide for the day's needs, as well as store leftover energy for the day food might not be found. As a result, they survived in greater numbers than their low-fat/low-sugar preferring neighbors—and they passed their genes along to us.

Should I cut out carbs?

You can try but you will never succeed. The only way to eliminate carbohydrates from your diet is to live on nothing but animal flesh and its products. Pretty much everything edible that grows is a source of carbohydrates. To eliminate them would require a very boring diet devoid of juicy apples, fresh-baked bread, hearty pastas, or zesty zucchinis…or French fries! Moreover, not only would your palate be bored to death, but your intestines would be too—so bored in fact that they would probably fall asleep (another way of saying you risk terrible constipation). Carbohydrates contain the fiber that helps keep your bowels moving.

However, if you are still hot to cool your carb intake and do not care about taste or going to the bathroom, also consider the functions that carbohydrates serve in keeping your body going. They keep your cells healthy and provide the fuel your brain requires to work properly. In fact, studies have found that severely restricting carbohydrates interferes with cognitive function, impairing memory and slowing reaction time[11]. Finally, imagine a world without garlic, honey, ice cream, grapes, asparagus, bread (or French Fries!) … boring!

What's the story on protein?

Protein is the third macronutrient (along with fat and carbohydrates) that we require for life. It comes primarily from animal products (meat, dairy, eggs), although some plants (e.g., beans, nuts, seeds, avocados) also have protein. It is needed to repair damaged tissue as well as grow new. Protein is essential to the production of enzymes and hormones, and to the proper functioning of our immune system (that last part is what keeps us from catching every bacterium and virus that goes around). Finally, when glucose (the sugar that is most easily converted to energy) is not readily available to our systems, our bodies can convert protein to a form of sugar that can be used to provide energy.

What should I cut out?

In the early 2000s, the Atkins Diet (a very low-carbohydrate program) had a resurgence in popularity. I had so many patients swear that everyone they knew was using it to lose weight and feeling great that I began to doubt my nutrition knowledge. After all, I am not a dietitian. So I called one of the smartest dietitians I know and asked her.

In response to my question whether Americans eat too much carbohydrate, my colleague replied, "Yes. And they eat too much protein. And they eat too much fat. They simply eat too much."

It is too much intake relative to movement that makes us overweight. So, eat all three macronutrients, enjoy the foods you enjoy, and balance them with movement.

How many calories are in each macronutrient?

Carbohydrate and protein each provide roughly four (4) calories per gram. Fat provides about nine (9) per gram. In other words, bite for bite you get twice as many calories from fat as you do from protein and carbohydrate. The easiest way to keep your caloric intake within weight-loss range is to decrease your fat intake.

The generally recommended macronutrient distribution is approximately 45–65% of your calories from carbohydrates, 20–35% from fat, and 10–35% from protein. To illustrate, if you were targeting 2,000 calories per day, this would translate into 900–1,300 calories from carbs, 400–700 from fat, and 200–700 from protein.

As you make your food selections, keep in mind that most protein sources, nuts, seeds, and grain products also include varying amounts of fat. Hence, while you can reasonably estimate about four calories per gram for fruit and vegetables, the calorie content of other foods will depend on the amount of fat each item contains.

And if your head is spinning from this answer, the important take-away is that there is no one perfect number of anything and your best strategy is to have your daily intake be mostly carbohydrates (e.g., vegetables, whole grain, fruit, rice) with the balance roughly split between protein and fat.

What are micronutrients?

Micronutrients are essential vitamins and minerals our bodies require. They are found in varying amounts in the foods we eat. When planning a healthy menu, if you incorporate adequate amounts of the macronutrients from a good variety of food, you are not likely to experience macronutrient deficiencies. If you do have concerns about the adequacy of your diet, please seek guidance from a Registered Dietitian.

What nutrients are in alcohol?

None. In fact, alcohol interferes with nutrient absorption and is converted by your body into fat. If you are trying to moderate your daily caloric intake, allotting a portion of your daily calories to alcohol is neither a healthy choice, nor one that will make it easier to manage your weight.

What is junk food and how do I avoid it?

In our common vernacular, junk food usually refers to high-fat, high-sodium, and high-sugar items. Foods found on most fast-food menus fall into this category because of their typically high-fat/sodium (e.g., burgers, breaded chicken, fries) or high-sugar content (e.g., milkshakes, flavored coffees, sauces, and salad dressings). Also grouped under the junk food heading are most of the snacks and desserts we love.

As for avoiding junk food, don't. There are few things that more consistently make us want, crave, desire, "die for!" something than being told we can never have it. Do not waste your energy on that useless effort.

The best thing to do about junk food is to include it in your life in planned, moderate amounts. If fast-food restaurants make your heart sing, go to them but less frequently than you have thus far. As for those high-fat/sodium and high-sugar snacks, either restrict them to when you are out (at restaurants, parties, etc.) or keep only small containers of them at home and plan when you will eat them rather than having them be impulse foods.

What is healthy eating?

Healthy eating in the 21st Century means eating *abnormally* relative to your design. It means not ignoring hunger signals until you are ravenous (so stop dieting!). It also means allowing satiety signals (or simply the fading of hunger signals) to prompt you to slow down and consider whether to continue to eat. To do this, it helps to learn about the foods you eat and how your body works. It means structuring your daily routine to minimize the impact of the mismatch between your body and environment, as happens when your body has had enough but the waiter brings out Death-by-Chocolate cake and you eat past comfort. Using your intellect to manage your social and physical environment is key to overriding that mismatch.

Am I addicted to food?

Good grief I hope so! As the discussion about fat, carbohydrates, and protein hopefully has made clear, if you stop eating, you die.

BODY

Understanding the interaction between food and your body will help you make decisions that support your weight management efforts.

What is metabolism?

Metabolism is the total amount of energy your body uses to maintain itself. Whether you require more or less energy (i.e., calories) depends on the interplay between your physical body and your environment, and that interplay is affected by your choices.

The energy required by your body to keep itself alive is your Basal Metabolic Rate (BMR). Ingesting fewer calories than required for BMR would result in body systems, such as your heart and brain, breaking down. However, over and above BMR, you need additional energy/calories to:

- Extract nutrients and energy from food. In other words, the act of taking in calories (eating) burns calories as you digest.

- Cool you down when environmental temperatures are high, and warm you up when they are cold. This is called *thermoregulation* and it burns energy.

- Maintain reproductive fitness. In other words, our bodies use calories to produce healthy eggs and sperm, and support pregnancies and lactation to produce healthy babies.

- Grow and repair cells/tissue. Here is where your body composition comes into play in moderating metabolic rate. Muscle requires more energy to maintain than does adipose tissue. So, increasing your muscularity tends to increase the number of calories you require just to stay alive.

All these functions use energy. In addition, the activities you engage in each day (such as thinking, talking, walking, making love, typing, texting, cooking dinner, to name but a few) also are fueled by the energy you eat. So, as you choose to walk rather than ride, or chop broccoli yourself rather than open a bag of frozen chopped green stuff, you increase the number of calories you burn. As you do more and move more, though, you require more calories to stay alive.

Can I change my metabolism?

You can *decrease* your metabolic rate, and thus more easily *gain* weight, by:

- Eating a very low-calorie diet or eating infrequently and inconsistently. Doing that causes your body to shift into miser mode and become very stingy about burning the calories you eat.

- Being sedentary so that you use less energy and do not maintain adequate muscle mass. Muscle uses more energy than does fat, so having more muscle means you burn more calories just being alive. If you are mostly sedentary, you miss out on the benefits of adequate muscle mass.

You can *increase* your metabolic rate, and thus more easily *lose* weight, by:

- Eating enough food to meet your BMR *and* most of your daily activity needs. If you eat a little less than your *total* energy requirement, you will lose weight.

- Increasing your overall level of physical activity via natural as well as programmed activity to burn calories while moving and benefit from the elevated metabolic rate that remains for a while post-activity.

- Increasing your muscle mass with strengthening (resistance) exercises.

Action Item

We will talk in greater depth about physical activity in Chapter 8—Exercise. For now, if you are serious about improving your overall health, begin to *gently increase your daily movement* with the strategy outlined here. It will help you move toward improved fitness without frustration, sore muscles, or having to re-arrange your schedule and sell your kids or pets in order to pay for a gym membership and personal trainer.

The equipment you need: A step-counter. You can use one of the electronic devices like a Fitbit™ or Apple Watch™, or simply an inexpensive pedometer that clips onto your clothes.

What you need to do :

1. Put on your step-counter each morning and wear it throughout the day—from wake-up to bedtime.

2. At bedtime record the number of steps you took that day. If you are using a simple pedometer, do not forget to zero the counter in preparation for the next day.

3. Repeat Steps 1 and 2 every day for a week until you have seven totals recorded. Graph these. (See Marta's sample below).

4. At the end of the week, add together the seven daily step counts and divide the total by seven; that is the mean (average) number of steps you are currently able to easily do. Set that number as your minimum daily target for the next week.

5. As each day over the next week draws to a close, if your step count is not at or above your target, stand up and

start moving until it is. Graph your total at the end of the day.

6. Repeat Steps 1 through 5 week after week. Each new week's minimum target will always be within your reach, but because you are working on staying at or above the minimum, that minimum target will gently increase over time. (Note: There is no need to go overboard. When you are averaging about 10,000 steps per day, consider it a win and shift your focus to maintaining it.)

Marta's sample graph of daily steps over 4 weeks

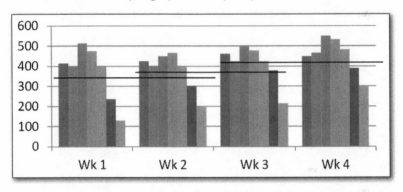

Look at Week 1 of Marta's graph. The black line across the seven daily totals is her average for that week (about 340 steps), and is drawn to extend out to become the minimum daily target for Week 2. Aiming at this target during Week 2, which Marta knew she could reach because of her activity during Week 1, pushed her to increase her average daily for Week 2 and she achieved roughly 360 steps. That average then became the minimum target for Week 3 and so forth. In this fashion, Marta gently increased her average daily activity week by week until she signed up for her first 5K walk (over 6,500 steps).

What is body fat?

The technical term for body fat is "adipose tissue" and it has a greater purpose than simply to annoy us and generate revenue for the local gym. In addition to cushioning our bones and organs and maintaining the health of cell membranes, fat also produces hormones critical to our ability to think, reproduce, and generally stay alive. It is also the place in which our bodies store energy not needed for living right now so it is available for living later[12].

In addition, fat serves as a storage site for several essential vitamins. It stores Vitamins A, D, E, and K which you need for the functions shown in the table below.

Vitamins Stored in Fat and Their Functions	
Vitamin A	Vision; bone growth; reproduction; cell division and cell differentiation; regulation of the immune system (fight off infections); surface linings of the eyes and the respiratory, urinary, and intestinal tracts; helps skin and mucous membranes function as a barrier to bacteria and viruses.
Vitamin D	Calcium absorption; bone growth, strength, and health; modulation of neuromuscular and immune function and reduction of inflammation.
Vitamin E	Protects cells against the effects of free radicals, which are potentially damaging by-products of energy metabolism; plays a role in immune function, DNA repair, and other metabolic processes; might help prevent or delay the development of cardiovascular disease and cancer.
Vitamin K	Helps the blood clot, prevents excessive bleeding.

Action Item

If you did not carefully read every word in the **Vitamins Stored in Fat and Their Functions** table, do so right now!

Do not skim, do not skip around, read each and every one. Then think about which of those functions you want to live without in favor of trying to ultra-minimize the fat you eat and the fat in your body. Perhaps you would be happy enough without being able to see, having the ability to fight off infection, or perhaps you do not care much about being able to stop bleeding when you nick yourself.

Odd as it may sound in our diet-obsessed culture, you can do yourself the greatest good by adopting the food mantra: "There are no bad foods, only bad quantities."

NOTE: In case you are tempted to choose being ultra-thin over any of these functions, let me assure you that I have worked with many patients who made that choice, and the result was catastrophic. Those individuals who did not die, profoundly regretted it.

Why do we make more fat than we need?

During the eons we wandered our planet chasing an unpredictable food supply, our bodies became increasingly energy efficient. Periods of hunger would cause our metabolism to slow so that we were able to store more of our food as fat for future use, and slowly break down that fat to release energy to stay alive until the food supply improved. When it did improve, our metabolism eventually returned to normal, but not without first hoarding as much of the newly attained food as possible to be ready for the next shortage. To this day, when we restrict food intake for extended periods, our metabolic rate drops, and our bodies fight to hold on to as much energy as possible.

If it is beginning to sound like biology has set us up to be overeaters who frequently binge and easily gain weight, you are getting the picture. We are indeed wired to be somewhat deaf to hunger and satiety signals and driven to eat when food is available. As insurance against periods of food scarcity, we are built to store as much energy as adipose tissue as possible and let go of that energy by breaking down fat in a slow, miserly fashion. This system worked pretty well for hundreds of thousands of years. The evidence of that is the fact that humans now blanket the planet.

How much can my stomach hold?

The average adult human's stomach can expand to hold roughly one quart of food and liquid. If you eat beyond that quart capacity, it can and does expand to accommodate your intake—to a point.

Once you are grown, your stomach size pretty much remains your stomach size. For the most part, you cannot shrink it by fasting, nor permanently stretch it by overeating. What you can do, however, is increase its elasticity by consistently overeating and train it to relax in preparation for accommodating large amounts of food when your brain signals that you have begun eating. However, your stomach does not remain over-sized and begging to be filled between eating episodes. If you are used to craving and eating large quantities, it is more because of your brain, than your stomach. Happily, your brain can be retrained. That is what we are doing now.

Does shape affect hunger?

Some studies[13],[14] have suggested that where on your body you carry excess weight can affect how well your brain is able to regulate hunger. Accumulation of excess belly fat may interfere with the brain's ability to recognize internal hunger and satiety cues—leaving you overly dependent on environmental cues to eat. What this means in our food-rich environment is that your belly fat may play a part in making it difficult for you to resist temptation even when you have eaten enough. Fortunately, there are simple strategies to compensate for this sensitivity. One is to practice focusing on your internal cues (see *The Stomach Exercise*), and others require your mindful attention to both the behaviors you do while eating and the way you structure your environment.

What is Ghrelin?

Produced in our stomachs, ghrelin is one of the hormones involved in signaling hunger. When this ghrelin-hunger link was discovered several years back, the media went crazy—trumpeting the discovery of the solution to obesity … if we could lower ghrelin levels, people would not be hungry and not overeat and obesity would be solved. Low and behold, some weight surgeries lower ghrelin levels (by reducing the amount of hormone-producing stomach surface) and so obesity is solved. Right?

Wrong—for two reasons. One is that ghrelin is only one of many hormones, enzymes, and other biological bits involved in hunger and satiety. The other reason is that hunger and satiety are only partly based in biology. A significant part of what drives our eating behavior is our psychology. Think about it—have you **never** chosen to eat more when you have been physically full? (Be honest with yourself.)

What is Leptin?

Produced by fat cells, leptin is a hormone that is involved in signaling satiety; elevated leptin levels have been linked to reduced hunger. Discovered in 1994, the media (and the medical world) became very excited. At last, everyone thought, we have a dial we can turn to decrease hunger and help people lose weight!

Wrong again—that was more than 25 years ago, and we are heavier than ever. Leptin, like ghrelin, is only one of a multitude of biological bits involved in feeding. Manipulating leptin does not appreciably affect our psychology and it is our psychology that primarily drives behavior.

How does dieting affect hunger awareness?

If you have a long dieting history, you have spent years training yourself to ignore bodily cues of hunger and satiety. In a word, your signaling system is shot. If you want to lose weight and keep it off, forget "natural" eating and design a reasonable schedule to follow.

BEHAVIOR

With a clear grasp of the essential nature of food and how it interacts with your body, it is now time to talk about what you should do, or minimize doing, to help yourself move forward.

What should I eat to lose weight and not regain it?

First, let me remind you that I am a psychologist, not a dietitian. If you have complex or medically-driven nutritional require-ments, make an appointment with a Registered Dietitian. Dieti-tians know more about food and its connection to health than you can imagine. That said, let me talk about the psychological side of deciding what to eat.

Regardless of whether you are a carnivore, herbivore, omnivore, or somewhere in between, there are three considerations you must incorporate into your food choices if you want to manage your weight for life:

- *Nutrition*—Regardless of the specific menu strategies you choose, they must include a broad variety of foods that provide protein, carbohydrates, and fat to nourish your body. Severely restricting any one of the macronutrients will damage you physically, as well as set you up for cravings for the foods that you have made off limits.

- *Satisfaction*—Select foods for the flavors and textures that please your palate. Following a meal plan with which your best buddy lost 100 pounds, but that forbids foods you like, may result in some weight loss but not *lasting* lower weight stability. When you are done with the unsatisfying plan, you will also be done with the weight loss.

- *Tradition*—Along with nutrition and satisfaction, be sure to respect the traditions that are meaningful to you. Swearing off Mom's apple cake that has been a beloved treat since you were a child, will only make you feel deprived and count the days till you are done with the diet. On the other hand, if you mindfully incorporate foods that evoke pleasing memories and emotions and complement special times, you can lose weight and have your cake too.

What menu plan should I follow?

If you have any condition that requires specialized nutritional guidance, please consult a Registered Dietitian or your physician.

If you do not require specialized guidance, I strongly encourage you to resist hopping on any diet plan. You have been there, and you have done that—low-carb, keto, no-white, gluten-free, North Beach, South Beach, raw, Atkins, blood-type, Beverly Hills, and the list goes on. Those may all be excellent plans for their authors, but they are not *your* plan.

The best plan for you is one that meets the three criteria of adequate nutrition, satisfaction, and honoring your traditions. The only way I have seen people lose weight and not quickly regain once they 'finish' their plans is by keeping an eye on their total caloric intake and meeting all three of these requirements.

How much should I eat?

By now it should be clear that you must eat enough to stay alive and not restrict your intake so much that you cannibalize your own flesh. The goal is to lower your intake just enough to begin slowly breaking down fat.

The best way to determine a target caloric intake is to figure out how many calories per day you currently average. To do this, review the last seven days of your Log, look up the approximate number of calories you ate each day, and then calculate the mean of those seven numbers (i.e., add the seven numbers together and divide by seven). This is your baseline intake.

There are generic recommended daily calorie intakes for adults but before you turn to generic guidelines, I encourage you to begin by figuring out where you currently are with respect to intake and gently reducing the amount until you begin to lose weight.

Action item

Review seven days of completed Logs to *calculate your average daily calories*. That is your **baseline intake**.

If during the baseline period you have lost weight, do not reduce your calories further; keep your intake at this level. However, if you have consistently lost more than two pounds per week for several weeks, consider increasing your daily intake by 200 calories. If you continue to lose more than two pounds per week over the next two weeks, increase your intake another 200 calories per day. The goal is to achieve a fairly steady average loss of one to two pounds per week. Hence, you may need to adjust your intake up and down 200 calories per day over several weeks to hit the target rate-of-loss range.

If during the baseline period you have gained weight or held steady, reduce your intake by roughly 500 calories per day for the next two weeks. If you lose one to two pounds per week, that is a good target intake for you. If you do not lose (or if you gain), reduce your intake by an additional 250 calories per day. If another week or two go by and you still do not lose weight, and you are sure you do not have a metabolic condition that is interfering, further reduce your intake by 250 calories per day. However, it is not recommended that women eat fewer than 1,200 calories and men fewer than 1,500 calories per day[15]. Doing so will make it less likely that you are receiving all the nutrients you need for health, as well as increase the likelihood that your metabolism will slow down and ultimately make it more difficult for you to lose and not regain.

Once you achieve a fairly consistent (not perfect) loss of one to two pounds per week, that daily caloric intake is your **target intake**.

Over time, if weight loss stops or significantly slows

down and you are sure that you are hitting your target most days and not binge-eating, you will make decisions about whether to further decrease your intake, increase your activity level, or both. If you find yourself stalling well above your target weight range even though you are hitting your calorie target and exercising most days, you may need to reconsider your target weight range. It is often the case that a weight plateau means you need to continue doing what you have done to arrive at that weight and allow your body time to get used to it. Continue at your current level of intake and activity for a few months and then reassess, possibly deciding this is a comfortable weight for you or opting to restart the process with a small additional calorie reduction.

If you are consistently hitting your intake and exercise targets, but not losing any weight at all, it is best to consult a dietitian or your physician before further tweaking your strategy. You may have something going on metabolically that is impeding your progress, or you may simply be miscalculating your intake.

As for what your target intake should include in the way of food, the answer is simple: variety to ensure adequate nutrients, flavor to make it enjoyable, and tradition to make your menu meaningful and satisfying for you.

Is there an easier way to figure out target calories?

Yes, although I strongly encourage you to use the gradual process outlined in the preceding Action Item. However, if you want more specific guidance, the following table shows the recommended daily calorie intake for adults who are in generally good health to maintain a healthy weight. *Sedentary* refers to a lifestyle that does not include any physical activity beyond that required for independent living. *Moderately Active* includes the activities of independent living plus the equivalent of walking 1.5 to 3 miles per day at a rate of 3 to 4 miles per hour. *Active* means walking more than three miles per day at 3 to 4 miles per hour in addition to the activities of independent living.

Estimated Calorie Needs per Day by Sex and Physical Activity[16]

	Sedentary	Moderately Active	Active
Females	1600–2000	1800–2000	2000–2400
Males	2000–2400	2200–2800	2400–3200

You can set your target calorie intake aiming for the higher end of the range relevant to you. If weight loss of one to two pounds per week results, stick with that target. If no weight loss occurs over two or three weeks at this level, set a daily level of 200 calories less for the next week. If no weight loss results, drop another 200 calories per day the following week. You can repeat this process until you begin to lose one to two pounds per week. However, do not target fewer than 1,200 calories per day if you are female, or 1,500 calories per day if you are male without consulting with your medical provider or Registered Dietitian.

What is the best eating schedule?

The right schedule for food intake is partly dependent on your membership in the human race and partly dependent on your lifestyle. As a human, it is reasonable to expect that if you eat "whenever," that *whenever* will be whenever food is in front of you. So, as member of our race, it is best to have a generally regular schedule of when you eat. In fact, scheduling food intake every two to four hours will prevent you from becoming so hungry that you lose control when you do eat. For most people that roughly means breakfast, lunch, and dinner, with a snack between at least two of them. That is the human race half of the answer to the question.

The lifestyle part of the answer is, you guessed it, dependent on *your* lifestyle. Work, school, and life obligations can make scheduling mealtimes a challenge and sometimes you have to be creative to make a reasonable schedule happen. In can be tough. However, if you need a motivating thought, consider this. Going many hours without food creates two problems for your weight. One problem is it lowers your metabolic rate so that your body burns fewer and stores more calories. The other problem it creates is Big Hunger so that when you do finally eat, you are more likely to make high-calorie choices and eat and eat and eat! In a nutshell, food restriction sets us up for overeating and not being able to efficiently burn those calories. Restriction (aka dieting) is fattening.

Three people, three schedules

Ronnie is an emergency room (ER) doc who works 12-hour shifts, some during what we would consider 'normal' and others during swing and graveyard hours. Hence, Ronnie is often working when others are sleeping, sleeping when most of us are eating, or just plain trying to catch her breath between patient surges. As you might imagine, planning three evenly spaced meals with scheduled between-meal snacks for Ronnie's schedule was more complicated than building the Mars Rover. So, instead of trying to force her crazy work schedule to accommodate the typical pattern of meals and snacks, Ronnie asked herself how she could ensure she ate a healthy amount of food as evenly spaced over her 12-hour shifts as possible? The answer she arrived at was to bring her day's worth of nutrition (i.e., for the 12-hour shift) packed in multiple small servings that could easily be eaten in spurts. Rather than try to force time for a 'proper dinner,' Ronnie brought enough food in small enough portions that even during those shifts that allowed her almost no down time, she was still able to have nutritious, satisfying food.

Bob teaches high school. His days are built around getting his own kids off to middle-school in the morning, corralling other people's kids through the day, and then chauffeuring his kids to soccer and band before organizing dinner, homework, bath, and bed. For the most part, he was able to structure the family's mornings and evenings to allow for a focused time to enjoy those meals. However, when I urged him to carve out a proper lunch time during the school-day, I thought he was going to hit me! (Not really ... Well, maybe really.) After educating me about the parent phone calls he returns, staff meetings, extra-help for students, grading, email obligations, and trips to the front office for paperwork the administration wants completed but forgot to give him in the morning—all tasks to be completed during his "lunch break," I withdrew my urging. Instead, we figured out a few workable lunch menus Bob could prepare on Sundays and rotate through the week. Each meal provided a good variety of nutrients, was easy to pack, required neither refrigeration nor heating, was filling, and easy to eat with one hand. Each morning, Bob would grab one of the lunches from his home fridge and store it in his desk drawer until the lunch-hour. While it was not a cordon bleu meal, it was filling, satisfying, could be eaten with one hand, and helped Bob meet his weight management goals.

As a retired accountant, Hannah found meal and snack

scheduling right up her skill alley. Although her days no longer had the structure imposed by the workday, it was easy to identify fairly regular times for her main meals. Eating breakfast later in the morning than she had during her working life, Marta seldom found herself hungry between breakfast and lunch, so she did not bother with a morning snack. She planned an afternoon snack for the 3:00–4:00 hour as that fell roughly between when she would have lunch and dinner. As for an evening snack, she found that as long as her intake was adequate throughout the day and through dinner, the evening munchies that plagued her before we began working together simply became a non-issue. Sometimes she would have an evening snack, and sometimes not.

Action Item

If your current daily eating pattern is erratic, **work on developing a more structured schedule** for yourself. It may take several tries until you settle on one that works for you, but it is well worth the effort. Also, keep in mind that you may need to build a few different schedules to accommodate your lifestyle if you have different obligations on different days of the week.

Action Item

If you have not been doing so, **begin recording the times you eat** in your Log. Having this information will help you trouble-shoot when you find yourself slipping, or weight loss slows. My patients often find that over-eating episodes tend to occur on days they have gone long periods without eating.

How can I learn to hear my body's signals?[17]

Physical signals of hunger and fullness (satiety) are not as clear as we would like. In fact, they are often difficult to detect. By the time your stomach is grumbling for attention, you are usually past the point of needing food. On the flip side, unless you are eating slowly, by the time you notice that you have eaten enough, you have likely over-eaten and need to loosen your belt.

Letting your body's signaling system help you eat healthy and satisfying amounts of food requires you to do two things. One is to eat often enough that you are not overly hungry and likely to overeat by the time your stomach finally gets your attention (see: *What is the Best Eating Schedule?*). The other thing you must do is slow down your eating speed enough to allow your body time to recognize the arrival of nutrients before you have cleaned your plate. Food does not instantly go from your mouth to your blood stream to your brain. It takes time. Everyone is a little different, but a reasonable rule of thumb is to assume about 20 minutes from your first bite of food before your brain gets the message that you are being fed.

What is the Mouth/Hand Rule?

The ***Mouth/Hand Rule*** is how you slow yourself down. It simply means that when there is food in your mouth, your hands should be empty. For instance, pick up your sandwich, take a bite, put the sandwich down, chew, and swallow. Then pick up the sandwich for your next bite. The same applies to using utensils to cut and spear bites; cut the food, put a piece into your mouth, put down the utensils, then chew and swallow before preparing the next bite.

Action item

Make the commitment to *use the Mouth/Hand Rule* for all eating from here on. It will take a good deal of attention before this becomes automatic so if you are comfortable doing so, ask your meal-mates to remind you if you forget.

The *Mouth/Hand Rule* means that if there is anything in your mouth, your hands should be empty. While there are times this will not be possible (eating an ice-cream cone comes to mind as an example), this should become your default eating style.

Why are you talking about the Stomach Exercise again?!

The Stomach Exercise is designed to help you learn to recognize your body's hunger and satiety signals. It is a funky exercise that typically makes patients wonder if they have chosen their therapist wisely, but it is effective.

Almost everyone to whom I have given this assignment has come back absolutely flabbergasted after doing it. Some are surprised at the discovery of hunger signals they would never have guessed existed for them. Others are surprised at their lack of noticeable signals—either of hunger or satiety. Almost all are surprised at what they notice as their fill-lines approach the top of the oval.

Action item

The Stomach Exercise: I will not say any more about this. If you have not already done it, do it!

Help! I don't have a volume control!

I know—not a question but nonetheless important. Some people seem only to have an on/off switch when it comes to eating. They are able to severely restrict their total intake or entirely avoid a particular food, but struggle or are downright unable to moderate intake. For instance, they are either completely off snacks, or they are snacking like there is no tomorrow. You can think of this like having a radio that either blares full volume or is completely silent. No volume control.

If this describes you, it is important to begin working on developing your moderation muscle. Begin by seriously committing to the *Mouth/Hand Rule* and renewing your commitment to your *Designated Eating Place* if you have been slipping. Doing so will slow you down and interrupt the automatic intake that is part of the problem. At the same time, be intentional about the portions you serve yourself, or allow yourself to be served. Put right-size portions on your plate and store the intended leftovers *before* you begin eating. Practice leaving a bit of food on your plate by pushing a small amount (about 5–10%) to a corner of the plate and not eating it. Silly as this sounds, it will actually help you weaken the link between see-food/eat-food as well as the link between empty plate/done. If you practice slowing down, right-sizing your portions, and not eating until everything is gone, you will find yourself increasingly able to moderate your volume (i.e., intake). This ability will not only make it easier to follow your plan but will make it much easier to occasionally slip without crashing entirely.

What are right-sized portions?

There are ample sources on the internet and on food package labels to teach you about recommended serving sizes for all the foods we eat. However, if you have been eating enough to become overweight or obese, or are still gaining weight, suddenly cutting your intake to the recommended amounts may hurt; and if it hurts enough, you are not going to keep at it.

Right-sized portions for you are slightly smaller than what you are currently used to eating. If your current intake is just a bit more than recommended amounts, go ahead and follow USDA Dietary Guidelines. If your portions are considerably greater, decrease them by about 10% until you get used to that, then decrease a bit more. Eventually, you will arrive at an intake level that works for your body.

Can I find joy in smaller portions?

Using the *Mouth/Hand Rule* to slow yourself down not only allows time for your body to experience the positive sensations associated with being fueled but combined *with No Simultaneous Activities,* forces you to pay attention to what is in your mouth. If you mindfully bite and chew, you will notice that flavors are equally tasty regardless of the size of the serving. Further, if you really pay attention, you will notice that as you become full, food does not necessarily taste as good as it did when you were hungrier. So, the answer is yes.

Should I use food only as a fuel source?

No.

Food is fuel, but oh so much more. Food is fun—it makes our taste buds happy. Food is social—we celebrate with it, mourn with it, flirt over it, show affection by sharing it. Food is also emotional medicine—sometimes milk and cookies or filet mignon are just what the pain requires.

There are many ways to meet the needs that food serves in our lives. To minimize overeating, it is important to develop multiple strategies to have fun, socialize, and soothe emotional pain. If you do so, having food as one of your strategies does not complicate weight management.

FOOD & HUNGER ROUNDUP

Your take-away from this chapter should be that the best 'diet' for you is one that fits your lifestyle, pleases your palate, and meets your nutritional needs. It leaves you neither hungry nor malnourished. Hopefully, you now understand that while there are unhealthy quantities of food, there truly are no bad foods. Incorporate your favorite flavors into your menu plan and eat multiple meals and snacks each day.

Action Step Recap:

1. Take the easy first step toward the physical activity you will need to create health and manage weight. Begin to *gently increase your daily movement* with the strategy outlined in this chapter.

2. Whenever you catch yourself recoiling at the word 'calorie,' remind yourself that *your body does an incredible amount of work* every single day of your life

and work requires fuel. Calories are fuel—calories are good.

3. Keep in mind that *we require a wide variety of foods* to get all the macronutrients (carbohydrate, fat, protein) and micronutrients (vitamins, minerals, and others we have not discussed here). Attempting to eliminate any of the nutrients we require will ultimately result in damaging your body rather than making it healthier or more attractive.

4. *Calculate your mean baseline intake and set a target intake that is slightly lower.* Your objective is to lose roughly one to two pounds per week. Refer to the detailed instructions in the relevant Action Item.

5. *Use the Mouth/Hand Rule* (i.e., hands are empty when food is in your mouth) whenever you eat.

6. If you do not already have a *consistent intake schedule*, devise one.

7. *Add 'time' to your Log* so you can monitor how well your schedule is working for you. By noting the length of time since your last intake when you overeat, you may be able to quickly resolve any emerging problems.

8. If you have not already done so, complete the *Stomach Exercise* during at least three meals over the next few days.

MAINTENANCE MINDER

Take a moment to think about what you have learned thus far and the steps you have taken. Whether you have implemented every single Action Item, or only a few, what you have done is worth celebrating and worth protecting. Weight management is not a race; it is a *style* that you are developing; a style that requires time and attention. Pat yourself on the back for what you have accomplished and decide what step you will take next.

Critical actions that you should prioritize, if you have not already implemented them, include setting a reasonable target weight range based on your *Personal Weight Profile* and recording your behavior in a Log. The Log is extremely helpful in identifying your *high-risk situations* and the *cognitive distortions* that interfere with your progress. Apply *Contextualize, Plan, Rehearse (CPR)* to your high-risk situations so you are better prepared to handle them when they occur. As you become aware of your cognitive distortions, develop rational rebuttals to prevent them from tripping you up.

If you have not yet done the *Stomach Exercise*, please do it. The exercise adds only a few extra minutes to your mealtime and has the potential to make a profound difference in your life.

As life's ups and downs bump you around, there will definitely be moments or days that the motivation you felt when you first bought this book is at low tide. Use the motivational material you developed in Chapter 4 to give yourself a lift when you need it. If you have not completed any of the Chapter 4 exercises, start with the *Pros/Cons Matrix* and *Motivational ICE*. As you have time, complete the others.

If you have been using your *Designated Eating Place* most of the time, and minimizing simultaneous activities while you eat, you are taking a tremendous step forward. If you have not begun these behaviors, today is a great day to do so. They will be a pain to initiate and handsomely reward your effort in long-term easier weight management.

FOOD & HUNGER FOR PARENTS

The most powerful thing you can do to help your children develop healthy relationships with food is to be a role model who has a healthy relationship with food. By structuring the household to make nutritious options an easy-reach, and including 'junk food' in moderate amounts, your children will develop healthy habits.

One of the mistakes I often see parents make is talking to their children about good and bad foods—"this food is good for you, but that one is bad." Please do not do that. There are no bad foods. Too much of anything is ultimately bad for us. Even those apples a day that keep the doctor away can bring the doctor running if we eat too many of them. The best message to send children is that there are foods that give us terrific energy and help us grow strong, and some that are not as helpful, so we eat less of them and more of the helpful foods.

When children ask why they cannot have seconds or thirds of 'junk food,' the correct answer is that while it is yummy, too much will hurt their tummy.

CHAPTER 7

EMOTIONS & HUNGER

What we did not talk about when I introduced the FOOD & HUNGER chapter is the emotional component of food choices. We do not eat only to fuel our bodies. We eat to soothe and stimulate and numb ourselves, to express love and punish one another, to make a statement and to avoid communicating. The bottom line is that emotions are an important aspect of our eating decisions.

Shortly after birth, we were fed. Following our entry into a relatively cold world, the comfort of warmth and touch was linked to flavor in our mouth and nutrients in our gut and bloodstream. Our biology and our learning history (experience) were linked together at that first post-natal feeding and remain inextricably linked to ensure that eating has emotional meaning for us.

This chapter explores the ins and outs of managing the emotional aspects of your eating behavior. The material is organized to first give you insight into the nature of the emotion-hunger interaction and then focus on practical steps you can take to manage that interaction.

AT THE CROSSROAD OF EMOTION AND HUNGER

When people talk about emotional eating, they are usually referring to the overeating that occurs when one feels badly. However, eating is also an integral part of human social inter-action. We show affection by sharing food, and sometimes punish by withholding it. We entertain ourselves and others with food and even use it to signal our social status. Accepting or rejecting food can be a way of letting others know how we are feeling, either about ourselves or them, and over- or under-eating is one of the ways we soothe or stimulate ourselves. In a nutshell, emotion is as intimately involved in our perception of hunger and satiety as is the size of our stomachs, our blood-sugar levels, and the activity of our hormones.

Why does stress trigger eating?

Uncomfortable emotions like stress, fear, boredom, and anxiety are natural eating triggers. Think again about our native environment. We faced basically two daily threats to our survival. One was the risk of not finding dinner, and the other was the risk of *being* dinner. The risk of food shortage triggered food-seeking and eating. The risk of attack triggered the fight-or-flight response as our nervous system kicked into high gear to fight off a predator or run like the wind!

If you are reading this book, I know that your stressors are neither about food shortages nor about being the prey of large carnivores. The problem is that your body only has one general stress response—arousal. Whether you are facing a food shortage, physical attack, bank overdrafts, boredom, or a psycho boss, your body responds by revving up your nervous system. In the old days (really, really old days), you would either have gone in search of food, fled, or fought, depending on the circumstances. Nowadays, the whole fight or flee thing does not work in most situations. Thus, we are left with food-seeking. Stress, for many of us, leads to eating.

Why do some people stress eat more than others?

Good question. Unfortunately, there is no one good answer. There are, however, a number of forces that come into play, some of which may be more relevant to you than others, and others that may be relevant at some time but not all times. Here they are:

- Although eating is certainly the primal reinforcer (i.e., the first thing that made you feel good after birth), there are other experiences that also feel good and can soothe us. Tempted as I am to say that there are universal soothers such as sex or gentle caresses, that would not be entirely true. Even the power of those assumed universals is modified by life experience so that one person's 'aahhh' experience could easily be another's 'argh.' The extent to which an individual relies on food for self-soothing depends on how many other self-soothing skills she or he has developed, and how well-practiced those skills are.

- Brain research suggests that people who tend to do more emotional eating may have a stronger pleasure response to food than those less prone to emotional eating[18,19]. In other words, frequent stress eaters may actually experience greater soothing when they eat and hence that behavior becomes a stronger habit. The frustrating aspect of this bit of information is that we do not know whether these strong responders are born this way or have had life experiences that make food so powerful a soother. Regardless of the reason, it is something to be aware of as you work on shaping your behavior.

- With our natural predisposition to increase food-seeking behavior when feeling stress, our sensitivity to stress determines how frequently we are exposed to that overeating trigger. Further, regardless of our actual lot in life, the way we look at things is a significant determinant of our sensitivity and hence of our stress level. The same experience can be felt as more or less stressful depending on how you think about it. If you are more generally a glass half-empty person, there will be many more stressors in your daily life than if you tend to see problems as opportunities for problem-solving.

Do I have Binge Eating Disorder?

We talked about the signs of eating disorders in Chapter 3. However, if you have episodes of overeating that feel wildly out of control, it is worth spending a moment on the specific question of whether you have Binge Eating Disorder.

Binge Eating Disorder (BED) is a psychological condition that affects roughly 30% of overweight and obese people seeking weight-loss treatment[20,21]. If you have BED, you will need to address it before you can achieve long-term weight management.

See a licensed mental health provider for an assessment for BED if:

- You have recurrent episodes of overeating during which

you eat an amount of food that most people would consider excessive under similar circumstances.

- During these episodes you *feel out of control.* You are not eating because you are hungry or this is a special occasion or your favorite food—you are eating because you cannot stop.

BED typically does not go away on its own—but it does respond well to psychological treatment. My two favorite self-help books for BED if you prefer to begin that way are: *Overcoming Binge Eating* by Christopher Fairburn, and *Crave: Why You Binge Eat and How to Stop* by Cynthia Bulik. If you do not experience an appreciable decrease in BED behavior within a month or so, seek a therapist who is trained in the cognitive-behavioral treatment of eating disorders. You do not have to live with this disorder your whole life!

Do cravings mean my body needs that food?

Sometimes.

Most of the time, probably not. There are rare cases where someone develops a craving for a nutrient that she or he is severely short of. However, in our food-rich environment, this is pretty rare.

When you have a craving, it is the result of some combination of the following:

- You are hungry.

- You are stressed or bored.

- Something or someone made you think of that food, which is one you like, and now it is stuck in your head.

(You can think of this as the food version of a song ear worm.)

- You have been trying to abstain from that food which puts it in the realm of the forbidden apple in the Garden of Eden—too good to resist.

Cravings and urges have all the power of ocean waves. They begin big and powerful and if you do nothing to feed them, they fizzle out.

What is distress tolerance?

Distress tolerance is the ability to experience emotional discomfort without attempting to make it go away. For people trying to minimize their emotional eating, this means being able to have urges and cravings but not act on them.

If you struggle with emotional overeating, I am fairly certain that there are types of emotional stressors (e.g., anxiety, loneliness) that you find very difficult to endure and that typically trigger an overeating episode. The cognitive distortions that usually underlie poor distress tolerance are emotional reasoning (e.g., I *feel* overwhelmed therefore I *am* overwhelmed and cannot manage this) and catastrophizing (e.g., This feels so bad it is killing me).

As you Log your food intake, also make note of instances in which strong emotion drives you to overeat. These emotions are high-risk situations that you will need to more actively manage in order to manage your weight. We will talk about specific strategies in the next section of this chapter.

What is delay discounting?

Delay discounting, also called time discounting, is an interesting phenomenon that can be an obstacle when it comes to managing urges. Whereas poor distress tolerance is about feeling like you cannot survive discomfort, delay discounting is more like mental gymnastics wherein you convince yourself that what you thought was important, really is not.

Briefly, delay discounting means the longer you have to wait for a reward, the less value that reward holds for you, especially relative to some other closer-at-hand reward[22]. In other words, you convince yourself that the further-out reward really is not that important to you anyhow even though you previously valued it greatly.

For example, if you are trying to resist a second helping of dessert today so you can achieve a target weight range further down the road, the longer time to your goal may make the goal seem less valuable than the immediate pleasure of the second piece of pie right now. A variation on this is the impact of having to say no to an immediate reward in pursuit of an abstract goal such as "health." Just as it is difficult to maintain our commitment to a reward that is some time in the future, working on an abstract goal also makes it difficult not to experience a decrease in motivation for the goal.

To some extent, we all engage in delay discounting with no ill effect. It becomes problematic when our delay tolerance is so short that it interferes with self-care. Indeed, shorter delay tolerances have been linked to obesity and related behaviors such as skipping breakfast and not exercising[23,24,25].

What are social overeating emotions?

As discussed at the beginning of this chapter, eating and its pleasant sensations are closely tied to everything social. Depending on your life history and current circumstances, anything from tender feelings to joyous celebrations to business negotiations to births and funerals may make you feel compelled to eat with abandon. As is the case for the more negative emotions, the information you record in your Log will help you know what challenges to plan for and how best to do so. Watch for social situations that are linked to emotional states that trigger overeating.

NAVIGATING THE CROSSROAD

Getting the upper hand on emotional overeating calls on all the skills you have been working on since beginning this book. You must identify your triggers and the self-talk and actions that are making it difficult for you to move ahead more smoothly (Log entries are super helpful). Then you must rescript the self-talk and develop new action plans that better serve your objectives. Finally, you must practice by mentally rehearsing your planned strategies so that when you find yourself in tough situations, you are prepared to navigate them more easily.

How do I fill my half-empty glass?

Shifting one's thinking style from glass half-empty to, if not half-full at least containing something valuable, is key to both stress management and depression treatment. There are many good self-help books on the subject which I encourage you to consult if depression and stress are significant problems for you.

For current purposes though, here is the gist.

- When you feel stressed or anxious, ask yourself what prediction you are making about the situation. Identify what negative outcome(s) you fear. For instance, if running a few minutes late to work really stresses you out, ask yourself what consequence you are dreading. Odds are that you fear severely disappointing someone and possibly getting fired and ending up living under a bridge on the wrong side of the railroad tracks! (I am only half-jesting by using such an extreme example. If you are totally honest with yourself and dig deep, you will find that your unstated predictions can be pretty dark.)

- Then consider the rational evidence that those outcomes are likely to occur. Ask yourself whether having been late in the past has resulted in someone losing all confidence in you and firing you? Chances are you have been late in the past without losing respect from others. It is also likely that even disappointing a supervisor has not resulted in loss of employment, nor is it likely that losing this particular job automatically dooms you and those you love to life in a homeless camp under a crumbling bridge.

- Finally, rescript your thought process from, "If I'm late, boss will lose respect from me and fire me and my life will be ruined" to "Running late today is a bummer but will not destroy the positive reputation I have developed with my hard work and usual punctuality, nor will it provide grounds for getting fired and being doomed to a life of poverty." Then pull out your cellphone, let your place of employment know you are on the way, and tune the radio to a good station.

NOTE: A few of my favorites self-help books for depression/stress: Feeling Good: The New Mood Therapy by David D Burns; Anxiety & Depression Workbook for Dummies by Charles H Elliot & Laura L Smith; The Happiness Trap: How to Stop Struggling and Start Living: A Guide to ACT by Russ Harris & Steven C Hayes.

Can I stop emotional eating?

Chances are slim that you can entirely stop emotional eating—as in *never again* turn to food for solace or celebration. Chances are very good, however, that you can increase your arsenal of non-food coping strategies sufficiently to reduce your over-reliance on food so that it no longer creates unhealthy weight gain.

How do I minimize emotional eating?

Minimizing the frequency and degree of emotional eating requires you do five things:

1. **Stay fueled**. Do not allow your fuel reserves to drop too low. Well before your stomach begins to make embarrassing noises or your head to ache, your fuel levels are dropping. Feed your body at regular intervals so that if emotions make you turn to food, you are not also physically starving and double-driven to eat.

2. **Be reasonable**. Remember that eating is a primal reinforcer. That means you may not find another activity that 100% replaces it as an emotional balm. Do not set yourself up for more stress and ultimate failure by setting the unattainable goal of *never* eating because of emotions.

3. **Be flexible**. Generate a *Behavioral Balms* list. That is,

non-food activities and things that you find soothing. Make the list as diverse as possible. Include things that can be done alone as well as those that require other people, activities in a variety of locations including home and work and/or school, those that are free and those of varying degrees of cost, and so on. The point is to have a lot of choices available when you find yourself in need of comfort or distraction.

4. **Be prepared.** Outline a plan for recognizing when you are about to eat because of emotional triggers and the steps you will take to remind yourself to refer to your *Behavioral Balms* for help tolerating the emotion. For instance, when you find yourself agitated and rummaging through the pantry, tell yourself, "Pause and Ponder!" and promise yourself that you can continue rummaging for food after you review your list and do one or more activity for at least 30 minutes.

5. **Stay aware.** Keep track of how you do with each potential emotional-eating episode. If you successfully use an alternate coping activity, pat yourself on the back and invest a few minutes to identify what you did to make this happen. If you do end up engaging in emotional overeating, spend some time figuring out just where you slipped, revise your plan, and try the revision next time. It usually takes many attempts before anyone is able to consistently implement new emotional coping strategies.

Action Item

Commit to memory, or to an index card, your smartphone, or tattooed to your forearm (just joking on the tattoo) the *five keys of minimizing emotional eating.* Stay fueled, be reasonable, be flexible, be prepared, and stay aware.

Action Item

Start working on your **Behavioral Balms** list. Even if you are 100% confident that you already know all the things that you would include, make the list anyhow! If you often succumb to emotional overeating, that tells us that you are not yet awesome at using those Balms in the moment. Having a written or typed or texted or tattooed on your forehead (still kidding) list does not guarantee you will use it in place of an emotional binge. However, it dramatically increases your odds of success. Do it. Now!

How can I handle urges and cravings?

The secret to handling urges and cravings of any sort is this: *Know they pass.*

No matter how over-powering they feel at the moment, if you do nothing to feed them, they eventually pass. So, when you find yourself "dying for" something, know that you will not die and learn to *ride the wave and surf the urge.*

It helps to think of the urge as an ocean wave that begins far out at sea, swells as it approaches land, crests, and breaks into tiny powerless bubbles as it reaches the beach. All that is left is water lapping at the shore and slipping back out to sea. When you find yourself thinking, "I'm dying for [your craving]," remind yourself that no has ever died for lack of [that item]. The feeling of "dying" is simply the wave cresting. Take a deep breath, do something distracting, and the urge will dissolve.

Action item

Increase the likelihood that you are able to surf the urges by preparing a rescue sheet titled *Ride the Wave* or *Surf the Urge*, with a subtitle of *No, I won't die for this*, and beneath that record a list of distracting enjoyable activities that do not require advance planning or other people—pull these from the longer list of *Behavioral Balms* you completed earlier.

Aida and the Grand Canyon

Aida struggled with chronic binge eating and our work was progressing very slowly. She left my office week after week with good strategies to resist her daily after-work binges but thus far had been unable to follow through. She described the sensation as gut-wrenching fear that if she did not binge, she would fall into a terrifying abyss from which she would never escape. At one particular session with Aida shortly after I returned from a vacation to the Grand Canyon, I shared with her my apprehension as I approached the lip of the Canyon. From the parking lot, it appeared the Canyon edge signaled a sheer drop. However, upon inching closer to the edge, a trail became visible. Although challenging, the hike down and then up again was workable with the skills at hand. For Aida, this imagery gave her the courage to allow the binge urge to crest without needing to run from it. As usual that evening after work she felt like bingeing, but for the first time in many, many years, she did not. The urge passed more quickly than she anticipated, and life took a happier turn for Aida.

Do records help emotional overeating?

Your Log is one of the most powerful tools you have. Recording the thoughts and actions that precede, accompany, and follow eating does several things for you. Most obvious is that recording your intake gives you an accurate snapshot of what you have eaten so you can more intelligently manage your nutritional balance and quantity.

With respect to emotional overeating, your Log provides the information you need to identify those situations that most often trigger emotional overeating. If you are tracking the context of your intake, you will be able to plan work-arounds for difficult situations and work on developing rebuttals to distressing thoughts. (Hint: Including notes about your thoughts and feelings immediately following an emotional overeating episode will provide a rich source of material for rebuttal development.)

Ronnie

Several times per week, Ronnie, the emergency room doc who figured out how to feed herself despite crazy work shifts, frequently found herself agitated and overeating when she got home from work. Her Log pages were nicely detailed but, even so, we initially had trouble identifying the eating triggers. Examining her intake and activities just prior to leaving work revealed no pattern. However, when we stepped back and took a broader view, we noticed that work shifts preceding Ronnie's nightly overeating episodes almost all shared two characteristics. One was that they were exceptionally busy and the other, obviously related, was that Ronnie ate all her meals and snacks on the run rather than in the doctor's lounge or at a desk. We knew this from the 'location' information on the Log; not using even a half-ass*d *Designated Eating Place* told us that the shift had been wild and Ronnie had not had a minute to catch her breath. That knowledge in hand, Ronnie put in place what she called an Emergency Kit for times she came home frazzled. The Kit was a cheap plastic box containing her list of *Behavioral Balms*, a scented candle, and her favorite herbal tea. She kept the Kit in her pantry and opened it before she allowed herself to pull out any food or go to the fridge. Ronnie's late-night episodes pretty much went away and, as an added bonus, the decompressing effect of using the Kit helped her fall asleep more easily after a rough work shift.

What gives a rebuttal power?

In the case of Ronnie (above), the trigger was simply exhaustion and lack of having been able to focus on her at-work meals well enough to feel like she had eaten. Hence, when she got home, she was tired, agitated, and feeling a little (or a lot!) deprived. That was not too difficult to figure out and her rebuttal focused on reminding herself that she loves her work, crazy days are part of what makes it exciting, and she had indeed eaten enough today even if it doesn't feel that way at the moment.

Oftentimes, the emotional trigger is somewhat more subtle. Developing an effective rebuttal derives from figuring out what underlying belief or catastrophic prediction about a situation is driving your response. For instance, getting on the scale at the end of the week and seeing that the number has gone up even a little bit can throw you into a tailspin that lands you in the pantry. If you stop and think about it, the rational response to having gained is not to go on an overeating spree. To the contrary, the rational response would be to review your food records and figure out what you did or did not do to make this happen.

Why do we go in the irrational direction?

Our tendency to irrational behavior can almost always be traced to problematic beliefs and catastrophic predictions we make about events. In the example of having gained weight during the week, the problematic belief may be that we are failures if we are overweight and the catastrophic prediction is that this week's outcome is proof we will never succeed. Bam! A couple digits on a measuring device and our life is a disaster!!! Good grief.

Which brings us back to how do you develop powerful rebuttals? If you have been making notes in the Context column of your Log, you should be able to figure out what beliefs and predictions are triggering you. Having done so, imagine yourself helping a dear friend dig him- or herself out of this mess by pointing out the irrationality of the thought and scripting a realistic and hence more helpful thought. For instance, you might replace "I'm never going to be able to manage my weight!" with "A few weeks of missing my target does not mean I will never get better at this. Weight management is a complex process and takes a lifetime, so this blip doesn't mean anything. What I need to do now is calm down and review my Log for patterns that might benefit from tweaking." Write that rebuttal directly in your Log where you will see it when you need it. Then proceed to problem-solve.

Action Item

Review your Log and the *Weight Loss Resume* you

constructed in Chapter 4, and reflect on your past behavior for evidence of unhealthy beliefs such as, "A bad week means a bad outcome," and catastrophic predictions such as, "I will never reach my goals." Think about times in the past you have attempted to get a handle on your weight, or any habit, and the kinds of thoughts you had in reaction to events that derailed you. Try to **nail down two or three of these distorted cognitions and write rational rebuttals** to them. Keep these handy and refer to them when you find yourself feeling triggered.

Can I increase my distress tolerance?

Yes. There are two components to distress tolerance. One is cognitive and the other behavioral.

Cognitively, you need to identify the distortion that is making the situation feel so unbearable for you. Usually, the cognitive distortion has to do with emotional reasoning and catastrophizing along the lines of 'this feels so terrible that it surely cannot be survived,' and another fallacy that we've not yet talked about which is the belief that we should not have to feel so bad. These misguided beliefs lead to desperate efforts (usually overeating) to escape the feeling. The rational rebuttals in these cases must first address the fact that we most certainly do have to feel this bad on occasion. In fact, one of the most powerful rebuttals my patients learn to use is, "Sucks to be me right now." With that simple sentence, you acknowledge that you feel lousy *and* it is temporary. You need not numb the feeling, merely wait it out. (Remember, discomfort is also a sign you are changing!) Add to this statement a rational rebuttal addressing the fallacy that because something *feels* too terrible to survive it is, and you are well on your way to increased distress tolerance.

On the behavioral side of the coin, as you calm your racing thoughts, you have the option of using your *Behavioral Balms* to distract and further calm yourself, practicing mindfulness in the moment (see below), or using a combination of both.

What is mindfulness in the moment?

In a nutshell, mindfulness in the moment is the conscious decision to calmly observe your internal state without evaluating, judging, or trying to change it. Simple as this sounds, it does take practice and a little structure to help yourself along.

To shift into mindful mode, take a deep breath, hold it for a moment, slowly exhale, and then focus on breathing deeply and slowly. Notice what is going on in your mind as if you were an outside observer and as you do so, describe that process while incorporating your rational rebuttals. For instance, you may think, "I am freaking out because [situation] and feel like I can't stand it but that is just a feeling and doesn't mean anything real. Right now it sucks to be me, but I am clearly surviving without fixing it with food. I'll just keep breathing deeply until I feel a little more calm and then do [from *Behavioral Balms*].

Can I stop delay discounting?

Yes. Faced with a desirable immediate reward, you 'forget' how much you desire the longer-term more important goal. Here are some strategies to help you refocus on the important health destination when faced with disruptive detours:

- Develop a brief phrase that you recite to yourself when you need a reminder that this temptation will feel good for a few minutes, but your health goals will feel good for a lifetime. For example, "This may feel good right now but protecting my health will feel good for life."

- Give yourself a time-out from making any choices by reflecting on your good fortune and naming ten things in your life for which you are grateful.

- Use ideas from your Behavioral Balms to distract yourself until the urge passes.

- Review the motivational aids you developed in Chapter 4—Motivation.

- Finally, forgive yourself if (when) you do give in to the temptation. Do not go down the What the Heck path. Use *CPR* to figure out what made this time so difficult and take the next step forward.

Can you simplify this?

Clearly, I was not lying when I told you the changes I recommend are "simple" but not "easy." None of the steps are complicated by themselves. What can be hard, though, is seeing how it all fits together.

The schematic below is one I devised for a lovely patient who had not lost weight following bariatric surgery. The primary problem was that food was her go-to for just about every emotional desire—pleasure, stimulation, comfort, peace, happiness, etc. Although there is nothing wrong with food being a source of all these things, when food is the *only* source of those positive experiences, the result is over-eating and excessive weight gain. To get from *Overweight* where food was her primary coping mechanism to *Healthy Weight*, she had to practice the behaviors you and I have discussed to decrease the power food had over her emotional state. She also learned to challenge thought patterns that interfered with her ability to cope with distress and assert herself. She used these skills to help herself establish a nourishing eating style and increase her connection to non-food-based sources of joy.

Overweight →	To get from Overweight to Healthy Weight →	Healthy Weight
Food = pleasure Food = stimulation Food = comfort Food = peace Food = happiness Food = nourishment	Identify and let body cues guide intake: • Stomach exercise • Mouth/Hand Rule Minimize cues that trigger eating: • Designated Eating Place • No Simultaneous Activities • Make high-risk foods less available Enhance nutritional status: • Include all macronutrients • Consistent intake schedule Minimize impact of cognitive distortions: • Develop rebuttals • Apply CPR to high-risk (difficult) situations	Food = nourishment Food = pleasure, stimulation, comfort, peace, happiness AND Friends, Activities, Prayer, Books, Nature, Movies, Family = pleasure, stimulation, comfort, peace, happiness

Do I need to manage happy emotions?

That depends. If you cherish happy moments and food is a pleasant part of those times without resulting in you feeling physically and emotionally uncomfortable, then no. You do not need to manage your happiness.

If you find it almost impossible to enjoy positive moments without overeating and then feeling bad about it, the answer is yes.

How do I manage happy moments?

As is the case with all high-risk situations, it helps to identify even the happy ones so you know when you are walking into a potential landmine, and then plan for them. Identification is helped by good Log records.

Planning entails developing rational rebuttals for the misguided beliefs that this moment would be less sweet without more food, and mentally rehearsing those rebuttals. Also, to the extent possible in different situations, take charge of those happy moments.

For example, imagine it is your birthday and friends have gathered to celebrate you with a lovely meal, tasty beverages, and a gorgeous birthday cake in your favorite flavor. You remember that you are trying to improve your nutritional habits and manage your weight so perhaps you should not finish everything on your plate and have two slices of birthday cake. However, your default mode is, "It's my birthday and I'll eat if I want to"; the cognitive distortion being that your birthday would be less happy if you ate less. The helpful rebuttal in this case is to challenge the belief that your birthday would be less wonderful if you did not overeat. You could tell yourself something along the lines of, "I can eat if I want to, but I really don't need to eat everything plus second helpings to know my friends care about me and that I am blessed to be celebrating my day with them. In fact, it would be more wonderful to begin my personal new year with a delicious and comfortable celebration." Then, use your voice to thank and refuse offers of more, and when you finish your first slice of cake, use your napkin to wipe your mouth and then crumple it on your cake dish to signal to yourself (and your friends) that you've had enough.

Please notice that the objective is not to remove food from happy occasions. The objective is to happily incorporate food in healthy portions.

EMOTIONS & HUNGER ROUNDUP

Perhaps the most important thing to learn from this chapter is that eating in response to emotional arousal of any kind is normal and inevitable. Where hopeful weight managers most often run into brick walls (i.e., lose weight but never keep it off) is when they strive to behave in a fashion contrary to their makeup. Just as you have no realistic chance of achieving long-term mainte-nance of a weight that doesn't fit your genetics and lifestyle, or sticking with a menu plan comprised only of foods that give you no pleasure, attempting never to turn to food for emotional solace is a recipe for failure.

The key to managing emotional eating is 'managing' it—not trying to eliminate it. Figure out what emotions inevitably lead to overeating and what situations most frequently trigger them. Explore other ways of soothing yourself and accept the fact that while none of them may give you the 100% fix you might get from a large dose of comfort food, many will give you enough of a fix that you can cope with the remainder of your discomfort.

As the triggers are activated and the urges crest, remind yourself of what matters most to your life, the irritation of the moment or your health and long-term goals? Use your Log to become an expert about your triggers so you are increasingly able to side-step them. Use the strategies you have outlined to arm yourself with *Behavioral Balms*, rational rebuttals, and the freeing knowledge that even tidal waves ultimately become nothing more than harmless bubbles on the beach.

Action Step Recap:

1. Remember the *five keys* to minimizing your susceptibility to emotional eating:

   (a) Stay fueled.

   (b) Be reasonable.

   (c) Be flexible.

   (d) Be prepared.

   (e) Stay aware.

2. Start a list of **Behavioral Balms**, activities and things that you find soothing. Be sure to include a good variety of entries so that regardless of whether you are alone or with others, have money or not, you can always find something that will help you in the moment.

3. Create a **Surf the Urge** or **Ride the Wave** document that includes a subset of your *Behavioral Balms* that are especially helpful when you face strong urges. Be sure to include as a subtitle on that form the reminder, "I will not die for this."

4. Write **rebuttals to the cognitive distortions** that have tripped you up in the past. In all likelihood, these distorted beliefs and predictions are recurrent and will trigger you again. Having practiced rebutting them will make it easier for you to catch yourself, revise your self-talk, and avoid spiraling out of control emotionally as well as behaviorally.

5. Do not forget to **pay attention to your reactions to positive emotions** as well as negative ones.

MAINTENANCE MINDER

Whether it has been a few days, a few weeks, or longer since you began this journey, please be proud of yourself. The fact that you are at this point in our conversation means you have invested more than just the money to buy this book. You have opened your mind to new ideas and refreshed old ideas, allowed yourself to consider new ways of doing your life, and made some small and some larger changes. To whatever extent you have modified your behaviors and attitudes toward weight and food and movement, the fact that you are still here means you are moving forward. As I have said in the past, weight management is not a race. It is a lifelong style of being and as long as you are engaged, you are here.

If you have become sporadic in maintaining your Log, now is the time to assess the impact of that slippage on your long-term goals. If you have been successfully eating a well-balanced and satisfying diet and losing a pound or two most weeks for several months, you may be able to continue moving forward without the Log. That is unless you just stopped logging this week and thus have no idea whether your progress will continue without it. In that case, if you are desperate to give up the Log, consider a gradual step-down. Instead of recording everything you eat, try recording only the time of each meal and snack, along with any significant relevant events. If over the next month or so at this reduced logging level you continue to meet your goals, then try cutting back further by logging only weekdays and skipping the Log on weekends (or vice versa). Again, give this a month or so to determine whether it has an impact on your behavior. If you find yourself slipping backward, recommit to the Log. If not, step down further. As you go forward, if you find yourself either hitting a weight plateau or gaining weight, the Log is your most powerful tool. Use it.

Core behaviors that will help you maintain progress achieved and keep you on the health path include:

- Embracing a *reasonable target weight range* and *enjoying a diet that includes all the macronutrients and that tastes good to you.* Moderating the amount you eat will ultimately be easier to maintain than sticking to a diet designed by someone whose taste buds do not match yours.

- Be sure to *eat at regular intervals,* at least three meals and one to three snacks daily.

- *Weigh yourself once each week and graph the weight.* If you notice an upward trend over two or more weeks, review your Log to figure out what has changed in your behavior that may be contributing to the gain. As you approach your target weight range, the slope of the graph should decrease until it flattens out within the range. Continue to weigh weekly even when you settle in your target range.

- Eat primarily at your *Designated Eating Place* and be mindful as you do so. That means minimizing atten- tion-absorbing simultaneous activities and using the *Mouth/Hand Rule.*

- Periodically update your *Pros/Cons Matrix* and refer to the letters and/or images you created to remind yourself what you are working for.

- Stay alert for cognitive distortions and high-risk situations that make things harder for you. Use rational rebuttals, *Contextualize, Plan, Rehearse (CPR),* and the stimulus control techniques we have talked about to make things easier.

EMOTIONS & HUNGER FOR PARENTS

As is always the case, the most powerful *teaching* we do as parents is by *living*. Our children learn more from what we do than from what we say. When it comes to teaching them how to actively manage their response to strong emotions, however, things can get a little tricky. On the one hand, our children benefit when they hear us think aloud to sort through difficult situations, and on the other hand over-sharing our emotional struggles with our children is not healthy for them, nor for our relationship with them.

As you practice challenging your cognitive distortions and improving your ability to tolerate distress, model these efforts aloud without sharing details that your children have no business being privy to. For instance, you can say, "I am feeling grumpy right now so I will take a few minutes to sit and take some nice deep breaths to calm myself down" without going into detail about whatever it is that is making you feel bad, nor into detail about what maladaptive responses (e.g., overeating, drugs) you are trying to avoid.

In terms of training emotional-coping habits that do not over-rely on food, that begins with being selective about how and when you use food as reinforcement for your children. While it is well within normal practice to reward children with food treats, make sure that you equally often reward them with praise, hugs and kisses, special activities with you and/or friends, privileges appropriate to their age, and so on.

Try to avoid, or at least minimize, using food as a band-aid for physical and emotional injuries. The natural impulse to do so is already in place given food is our primal reinforcer. As Mom or Dad, your job is to help your children develop additional coping strategies. It is never too early to begin modeling soothing self-talk and guiding them to take a moment, catch their breath, and think about a useful solution to the problem at hand. (All in age-appropriate terms, of course.)

You want your children to grow up enjoying food *and* having other powerful tools in their self-soothing toolkit.

CHAPTER 8

EXERCISE

If anyone tells you that you must feel the burn, sweat blood, or hit a specific number of heart beats per minute in order to enjoy the health benefits of exercise, politely smile and ignore that person. The only exercise that will give you the health and healthy-weight benefits associated with exercise is exercise you *do*. In other words, movement that is somewhat (not extremely) easy to do or just plain fun or both. Further, the fact that weight management *does* require exercise means it is essential that you either find physical activity you enjoy, or figure out a way to consistently do activity that may not ring your happy bell but is tolerable. Happily, this need not be as difficult you think.

I have organized this chapter in two broad information groupings. The first section focuses on the *What and Why* of exercise—what it is, why it matters, what interferes with it, and its impact is on our bodies. The second section targets *How* you get going, keep going, and regroup when you hit bumps in the road.

WHAT AND WHY

Over 80% of Americans do not meet physical activity recommendations[26], and a comparable percentage of my patients over the past several decades came to me believing that the only exercise worth doing was that which they found impossible to keep doing. Hence, my dear reader, I am comfortable beginning this section with the assumption that you can benefit from a discussion that spans the basics to the sophisticated. If you are among the minority of individuals who already has a solid grasp of this material, my apologies for the repetition, along with encouragement to read it anyhow; it never hurts to remind oneself of what one knows.

What's the wheel got to do with it?

Based on diagrams on ancient clay tablets, the earliest known use of this essential invention was a potter's wheel that was used at Ur in Mesopotamia (part of modern-day Iraq) as early as 3500 BC. The first use of the wheel for transportation was probably on Mesopotamian chariots in 3200 BC.

(From: http://www.ideafinder.com/history/inventions/ wheel.htm)

Over the past 5,000-plus years, we have perfected the art of walking less. Along with that, we have also decreased our need to run, trudge, hike, amble, meander, saunter, trek, promenade, prance, stroll, ambulate, and march. In other words, the invention of the wheel has decreased the number of calories we burn going about our daily living. Subsequently and unfortunately, other inventions have increased the number of calories we can mindlessly get our hands on.

What is exercise?

According to dictionary.com exercise is "bodily or mental exertion, esp. for the sake of training or improvement of health."

In the old, very old, days we had no need of exercise. We did plenty "bodily exertion" searching for food and getting from place to place. In fact, even only 100 years ago we did not need much in the way of intentional, structured exercise because few of us owned cars and feet were our primary mode of transportation. Today, however, few of us use feet to get around and fewer still hoe, rake, plough, and otherwise exert energy to get food. As a result, we do need to intentionally include physical activity (i.e., exercise) in our daily patterns if we want to remain healthy and avoid obesity. For these purposes, exercise can be defined as *moving*. Stand up, walk around, jiggle your body parts, lift things, stretch up, and reach down. That is *exercise*.

What's it good for?

Moving is as much a part of being human as is thinking, drinking, eating, sleeping, and emptying one's bowels. Eliminate any one of these from your life and you eliminate your life.

In fact, exercise affects virtually every component of your body and hence affects your health, abilities, and appearance. The **Impact of Exercise** table gives you an overview of how exercise improves body functions and the impact those functions have on your health, abilities, and appearance.

Impact of Exercise			
Body Aspect	Health	Ability	Appearance
More muscle	Reduced risk for disease	Greater strength, mobility	Firmer body
Enhanced metabolic rate	Improved utilization of nutrients		Assists in weight management
Stronger muscles	Better skeletal support, lower risk of falls and fractures	Greater strength	Improved posture, smoother body contours
Stronger bones	Reduced risk of fractures and osteoporosis	Participate in life without fear of injury	Protects height, strong posture
Cardiorespiratory endurance	Greater cardiac health	Comfortable participation in activities	
Improved circulation	Lower risk of varicose veins, heart disease, light-headedness		Enhanced complexion
Lower cholesterol	Reduced risk of heart disease and some cancers		
Lower blood pressure	Reduced risk of heart attack, stroke, and kidney failure		
More energy	Easier to be active and enjoy greater health benefits	Ability to participate in life's pleasures	Walk and posture project more up-beat personality

How much exercise do experts recommend?

Most nations around the globe, including the United States[27], Canada[28], and the United Kingdom[29], have adopted the World Health Organization's (WHO) recommendations for physical activity[30].

For adults, the WHO recommends that each week we do at least 150 minutes of moderate-intensity aerobic physical activity, or 75 minutes of vigorous-intensity physical activity, or an equivalent combination, in bouts of at least ten minutes or more. Additionally, muscle-strengthening (i.e., resistance training) activities are recommended on two or more days each week.

Examples of Moderate-intensity and Vigorous-intensity Physical Activities	
Moderate-intensity Activities Moderate effort, noticeable heart rate increase.	Vigorous-intensity Activities Large effort, rapid breathing, substantial increase in heart rate.
• Brisk walking • Dancing • Gardening • Housework and domestic chores • Traditional hunting and gathering • Active involvement in games and sports with children/walking domestic animal • General building tasks (e.g., roofing, painting) • Carrying/moving moderate loads (< 40 lbs.)	• Running • Walking/climbing briskly up a hill • Fast cycling • Aerobics • Fast swimming • Competitive sports and games (e.g., football, volleyball, hockey, basketball) • Heavy shoveling or digging ditches • Carrying/moving heavy loads (> 40 lbs.)

You can achieve 150 minutes weekly by exercising 30 minutes on five days each week, or just over 21 minutes on seven days per week, or any other breakdown. The key is to accumulate 2.5 hours (that's 150 minutes) over the course of a week. That can be done in large or small chunks—whatever works best for you.

These recommendations target healthy adults aged 18–64. If you have a chronic condition that affects mobility or your ability to breathe, adjust your goals accordingly. Seeking guidance from your physician as well as assistance from a personal trainer is recommended in these cases.

NOTE: Please do not set your exercise goals before reading the answer below to "How much exercise do I need?"

What is aerobic exercise?

Aerobic exercise is any activity that causes your breathing and heart rate to increase over your resting rate. Also called 'cardio,' aerobic activity examples include walking, cycling, jogging, dancing, jumping, swimming, enthusiastic vacuuming—basically any whole-body movements that make you breathe a little harder and raise your heartrate.

Please note that is it is not necessary for you to be gasping for air and sweating gallons in order for the activity to count as aerobic. In fact, while doing moderate aerobic exercise you should be able to talk fairly easily, but not necessarily be able to sing. If you are unable to talk while exercising, you are over-doing it.

What are strengthening activities?

These exercises build your large muscle groups. Also called 'resistance training,' they include any action with which you either push, pull, or lift something; that "something" can be weights or your own body weight. It is worth noting that many aerobic activities also build muscle strength. However, aerobic activities tend primarily to work muscles in your lower body (e.g., legs) so it is important to give some thought to upper-body strengthening.

How much exercise do I need?

That depends on what you want to accomplish. If you are hoping to compete in the next Olympics, quite a lot. Much less if what you want to do is increase your fitness level, lose some weight, and make it unlikely that you will gain weight.

The WHO recommendations we reviewed above are for the generic, basically healthy adult, and represent good long-term goals to shoot for. However, unless you are very close to hitting that level of activity, it is best not to worry about them for now.

Right now the amount of exercise you need is slightly more than the amount you are currently doing. Begin where you are and move on from here. In other words, if you can walk for three minutes with a little exertion, do that. Do it every day until those three minutes are easier. Then add 30 seconds and repeat. When those 3.5 minutes get easier, add 30 seconds again and repeat. As your time gets longer, you can increase the size of your increases, but never add more than you can do with just a little more exertion.

Whatever activity you choose, do as much as you can with a little exertion, and do it until it becomes easy. Then increase your time and/or intensity in small bits. This way, you will gently increase your fitness level without making yourself hurt. How far you go with this is up to you.

Marta's Walk to 5K

Remember Marta, the gal who scoffed when I told her that eating more during the day and recording her intake would help her lose weight? The other thing she didn't believe would help was my first exercise recommendation.

Marta had a treadmill that had been standing in a corner of her bedroom for a few years. She had used it religiously for several days right after she bought it and, since then, it had served her very well as a clothes rack. Her first exercise assignment was to clear the clothing off the treadmill. It took a couple of weeks of repeating this assignment before she finally did it. Having achieved that success, her next assignment was to walk on the treadmill at a slow pace for one minute every weekday for the next week. It took another few weeks for Marta to (remember to) hit this target. Once she did, and felt pretty pleased with herself I might add, we increased her daily target to 90 seconds. This was easier; she hit it the first week and also reported that she went over the target a few times.

Over the course of the next few months, we increased Marta's weekdays target from 90 seconds to two minutes to 2.5 minutes to three minutes; then to five minutes, then seven, then 10, and so on. She also slowly increased her speed. Small increases meant Marta could always achieve the target without pain. About six months after clearing the laundry off her treadmill, Marta reported that she had signed up for a 5K fundraiser walk—which she completed!

What is Natural Activity?

Natural Activity is my favorite part of the exercise equation. I love it best because it is the easiest way to increase fitness. Simply, Natural Activity is the movement that gets you through your day. Walking from the bus or your car to your home or workplace, getting your mail, cleaning your home—all movement "counts", and all movement can be enhanced.

For instance, rather than park in the space nearest the door, park a few spaces or a row or two away. At the supermarket, thank the bagger who offers to push your cart to the car and do it yourself. Take the stairs instead of the elevator. Instead of swinging by the mailbox in your car, park at home and walk to the mailbox. You get the picture.

If you have been gradually adding daily steps as we discussed in Chapter 6, you will find that added focus on Natural Activity provides a huge boost toward reaching and advancing your step goals. The small increments of energy expenditure that come with increasing Natural Activity add up over time. If you are trying to manage your weight, Natural Activity is your friend!

What is my exercise goal?

If your hope is to promote weight loss and improve fitness, then your exercise goal is to increase the amount of physical activity you do over your current level. To get there, I recommend you begin with a *long-term* goal of achieving the WHO recommendation of 150 minutes per week of moderate-intensity aerobic activity, and two or more bouts of strength training each week.

However, we can only begin where we are which means that you need intermediate goals that are realistically achievable soon enough to be satisfying. The first step is to determine what you are capable of doing right now and *do it*. If your current capability is a three-minute slow stroll around your living room, then your first goal is to stroll 3½ minutes around your living room every day until that becomes easy. Then increase it to four minutes and repeat daily until you can increase it a bit more. The same strategy goes for strength building. Your initial goal will be to lift/pull/push as many pounds, or ounces, as you can with a little exertion, and as that gets easier, increase the target number of repetitions and/or poundage, or ounces if that is where you start, little by little.

Action Item

Decide what your ***first exercise goal*** is. Make sure it makes sense given your fitness level at this very minute. If you have been mostly sedentary until now, work on increasing your *Natural Activity* and adding steps to your day. There are wonderful health and mental health benefits to be gained from simply walking most days. When you are ready to up your game, do so in small increments so the increase makes you feel empowered rather than exhausted.

If you are already relatively active and want to take your fitness to the next level, consider consulting a qualified personal trainer (or your physician). If you prefer not to use professional assistance, the same strategy applies as outlined above—remember Marta and go slow! But go!

HOW

Knowing why exercise matters and what qualifies as exercise is an essential first step. It is also the easiest step. More difficult, is figuring out what sort of exercise you are ready to do and how to keep doing it.

Where do I find time to exercise?

In your typical day. Yes, that is correct. It is in your typical day. The belief that we are simply too busy to exercise has no more truth to it than the belief that double-fudge chocolate-chip cookies have negative calories if eaten while standing.

In 2019, a compelling study[31] that analyzed time-use data from over 32,000 Americans aged 15 and older found that we have more than ample time on our hands. In fact, on average we have even more free time than would be healthy to devote to exercise—more than five hours per day!

Hence, after decades of telling patients who argued they could not *find time* to exercise that, "No one has spare time laying around waiting to be found. We have to *make* time," I stand corrected. The time is there. Decide what you can do with it that best gets you where you want to be in life.

Can you give me ideas for Natural Activity?

I thought you would never ask! Here are 50:

1. Ride a bicycle before lunch or after dinner or ...

2. Take a walk after breakfast or before lunch or ...

3. Use a treadmill before turning on the television or watch while walking on treadmill.

4. Climb the stairs instead of riding the elevator.

5. Walk down the stairs instead of using the elevator.

6. Plant a garden.

7. Rather than phone, text, or email, walk to your co-worker's desk or office to communicate.

8. Park your car a block from your destination.

9. Find the furthest parking space in the lot and use it!

10. Rather than save all the things you need to bring upstairs for one trip, make three or four trips.

11. Walk the length of the mall once or twice before you begin shopping.

12. Use half your lunch break to eat and the other half to stroll outdoors.

13. Plan two-minute breaks every hour to stand up, stretch, and walk around the room. Set an alarm to remind yourself to get up.

14. At work or school, use the restroom at the far end of the building or on another floor.

15. Mow your lawn more regularly, not with a riding mower.

16. Offer to be your family's Chief Snow Shoveler.

17. When you take your children to the swimming pool, get in.

18. Use work breaks to go outside for fresh air.

19. If you want a donut, walk to the donut shop.

20. Take your kids to the playground and push them on the swings and merry-go-round.

21. Walk/explore your neighborhood. Then explore a neighborhood further away.

22. Vacuum your home an extra time each week. (Your carpets will benefit as much as your body!)

23. Lift light hand weights while you watch television.

24. Join a line-dance or folk-dance group.

25. Get off the bus one or two stops early.

26. Walk to the next bus stop before getting on the bus.

27. Rake the leaves on your lawn—and then jump in!

28. Rake the leaves again.

29. Join a square-dance club.

30. Walk instead of drive to lunch.

31. Take your dog for an extra walk each day.

32. Learn to tap dance.

33. Join a bowling league.

34. Coach a children's sport team.

35. Volunteer to walk yard duty at the local school.

36. Stroll your neighborhood before dinner.

37. Learn to ballroom dance.

38. If you live in an apartment complex, use the laundry room furthest from your apartment.

39. Volunteer for community clean-up events.

40. Ride a stationary bicycle while you watch television.

41. Use your stair-stepper while you watch a movie.

42. Hook a bookrack on your stationary bicycle and ride for one chapter.

43. During television commercials, do stomach crunches.

44. Walk the long way around to your destination in department stores.

45. Avoid escalator lines by using the stairs.

46. On moving sidewalks, walk.

47. Walk around moving sidewalks instead of on them.

48. Put your lawn chair indoors and take yourself outdoors.

49. Give your car a day off each week and get out of the house.

50. Fidget!

You can probably turn this list of 50 ideas into 500 by adding activities you enjoy, or simply need to get done on a regular basis. The trick is to spot opportunities for action in the many situations that make up each day. For instance, if you are at the computer and need to rest your eyes for a moment, you have two choices. You can close your eyes for a minute, or you can stand up and do five leg lifts while you look out the window. Both choices will rest your eyes but only the second will make you feel good all over.

Action Item

Decide on three *Natural Activity* opportunities that you will incorporate into every day, and two additional ones that you will add to your week. Use your Log to keep track of them.

For instance, you might decide to park in the last row at the supermarket, get off the elevator one floor early and climb the final flight, and take your dog out for an extra walk each day. Additionally, you might sign up for a bowling league that meets once per week and commit to mowing an elderly neighbor's lawn once each week.

Should I Log my activity?

Even if you already have a long-standing active routine that is as much a part of your lifestyle as is brushing your teeth, tracking your activity is helpful. Doing so gives you visual validation of your efforts and helps you trouble-shoot if you start slipping. (Yes, I know I'm repeating myself, but this is so very important!)

Action Item

Record your activity in the Context column of your Log or add a column explicitly for exercise. However you decide to track it is fine—as you long as you do track it.

Greg's Missing Willpower

Greg had gotten into the habit of taking a walk after dinner most evenings. At first it was difficult for him to leave his comfortable chair and put on his shoes, but he made himself do it and eventually came to look forward to his evening strolls. Lately, however, he had started skipping his walks and flopping down in front of the television instead. He still believed the walks to be important to his health but skipped them anyway. Asked why, he said, "I've lost my willpower."

When Greg looked at his Log, *he found his willpower.* Reviewing his Log pages for the period during which he began skipping his walks, Greg noticed that the missed walks were almost always on evenings he ate a late dinner. By the time dishes were cleared, he was simply too tired to move. Obviously, it was not willpower but timing that was the problem here.

With Log Sheet information, the solution is often simple. Since timing was the problem, a schedule change was the solution. If Greg could not plan earlier dinners, he could walk before eating or leave the dishes until after his walk. If neither of these solutions were going to work for him, he could plan ahead for late days by scheduling the walk earlier in the day.

How do I keep it going?

Think about routines, exercise or otherwise, that you have tried to establish in the past but failed to maintain. Invest the time to sort through how you went about starting them and what you did to keep them going for however long you did. Also think about what people, events, moods, or environmental changes interfered with maintenance. Be brutally honest with yourself—how much of the reason you stopped was due to your natural tendencies or personality, and how much was due to forces outside yourself? Then plan ahead for how you will handle those outside forces, and what personal quirks (mood or thoughts) you need be on alert for and how you can work around those landmines.

In addition to trouble-shooting strategies that are unique to your particular circumstances, my experience dictates that you must absolutely also include these three tactics:

1. Add physical activity tracking to your Log. This visible record of your efforts will help you trouble-shoot unexpected challenges, as well as recognize your progress.

2. Edit your description of yourself (i.e., your self-talk) from someone who is *trying to* establish an activity routine, to "This *is what I do*." The difference between the two thoughts is that someone 'trying' may or may not make because it's not really a part of who they are, and the "what I do" person does it.

3. Identify the landmines that typically throw you off your plan and plan for them.

Action Item

Map your exercise landmines. Having reflected on past exercise efforts and what sort of landmines blew them up, on a blank document draw four columns labeled *Event*, *Thought*, *Outcome*, *Plan*. Under *Event*, list the events that impaired your effort. For example, in this column you might list having taken a vacation during which you did not have access to a reasonable space in which to exercise. Then skip to *Outcome* where you would note that you never got back into the routine after returning home.

With *Event* and *Outcome* completed, double-back to the *Thought* column and think deeply to identify what you told yourself (i.e., the self-talk, distorted cognition) that turned a terrific vacation into an abandoned goal. Without knowing you personally, I cannot guess what your thought process was. However, I can tell you what the top three thoughts reported by patients are: (1) I don't exercise anymore, (2) I hate having to start over, and (3) I knew I wouldn't be able to keep it going. As you can see, it was not the lovely vacation that stopped the exercise routine; the vacation merely interrupted it for a few weeks. What stopped it was the individual's self-talk. If she doesn't exercise anymore, she does not exercise. If he hates starting over, that makes it pretty hard to get excited about it, just as knowing (not fearing, *knowing!*) she would stop makes resuming a non-starter.

Now move on to *Plan*. This requires a two-pronged approach. First, consider what structural or environmental safeguard you can put in place. For instance, during vacation you might intentionally increase your Natural Activity by tracking steps or making a game of it with your travel partner. With respect to the distorted cognitions, the key is to edit your self-talk. As I said earlier, you must edit your self-description from someone trying to develop this activity routine to someone who does this. Hence, the three thoughts my patients report would be revised to: (1) didn't exercise these past two weeks and am ready to resume now, (2) Starting over sucks but I've done it before so here I go, and (3) Of course I can keep it going; just watch me!

Best first step?

If you have been sitting on your sofa for the past year, stand up and walk around the sofa. Do this at the half-way and end of each show you watch, or after every article or chapter you read. After a week or so as the sofa route becomes too easy (or boring!), add a walk into and back from another room of your home until you can walk all over your house multiple times each hour without fatigue. This is the first step of your new fitness routine.

If you have not spent the past year on your behind, or after you have mastered the house-walk, set daily Natural Activity targets; each of which constitutes increased activity over your baseline but not enough to make you huff and puff. For example, park a few spaces further, use the stairs for the first floor before getting on the elevator, take steps on the escalator (or take the stairs instead), walk to the next bus stop before climbing aboard, dance in the living room.

If you are already reasonably fit, keep doing what you are doing and increase or add to it in small increments. For instance, if you have been walking one mile in 30 minutes every morning, push yourself to complete the mile in 28 minutes and do that daily until it becomes easy. Then either keep walking at that pace for your original 30 minutes or push to complete the mile in 26 minutes. As each new target becomes easier, increase it a tad.

My Personal Story

In an effort to interrupt the daily buildup of stress during a particularly stressful period of my work life, I began walking during lunch. A co-worker talked me into running with her. Initially, I could run only about 50 yards before I was gulping for air. So each day, I ran the 50 yards and walked the balance of my mile goal. When the 50 yards became easy, I added 10 steps and ran that distance until it became easy. Then added 10 steps, and when the distance became measurable in miles, increased ¼ mile at a time and so on. Within the year, I ran my first 10K and continued to enjoy running for many years.

What if I hate my new routine?

Change it. The only right routine for you is one that you get some pleasure or satisfaction (or at least minimal boredom and absolutely no pain) from. If the routine you initially decide on turns out to be a disappointment, do something else. If that becomes disappointing with time, change it up again. The only critical aspect of your routine is that you do it—whatever it is today.

EXERCISE ROUNDUP

The two most critical takeaways from this chapter are that getting enough physical activity to keep you healthy requires your attention and intention. Our modern world is simply not designed to make exercise a no-brainer. Unless you earn your livelihood digging ditches or lifting Volkswagens, ensuring you move enough to support your health means making the decision to make it happen. Whether you do that with natural or structured activity is up to you—but do it you must.

The other key takeaway is that the only starting place that will lead to your goal is where you are right now. No matter how brilliant and guaranteed and phantasmagoric an exercise program sounds, if it is not reasonably easy for you to do and at least interesting, or not boring if not enjoyable, it will not help. Decide on something that you can do with a little bit of effort that either holds your attention or allows you to concurrently do something interesting long enough to complete it. If that activity stops working for you, for any reason, move on to the next.

Action Step Recap:

1. Set an ***initial goal*** of increasing your current fitness ability by doing a little more exercise than is currently easy for you to do. As your stamina improves and this amount of exertion feels easier, increase it slowly.

2. ***Begin tracking*** your activity in your Log. Either use the Context column or add a column for exercise.

3. Increase your daily movement by incorporating three new ***Natural Activity*** opportunities into each day, and an additional two into each week.

4. ***Map your landmines*** by identifying circumstances that have blown you off course in the past and figuring out what it was about them that tripped you up. Enter the information in columns labeled Event, Thought, Outcome, and Plan. Describe the Event, record the Outcome, then double-back to figure out what you thought, said to yourself, about the event that resulted in the outcome. Finally, figure out a healthier way to handle that event in the future, and write it under Plan.

MAINTENANCE MINDER

This is our final Maintenance Minder. However, it is not the final time you should be thinking about maintenance. From the very first step you took to the very last breath you take, caring for your body and paying attention to your thought patterns and the behaviors that help or hinder is crucial to good health and lifelong body comfort. Regardless of how consistent you have been in practicing the strategies we have discussed, the fact that you are still attending to this means you have progressed, and that progress is worth maintaining.

Along with the Action Steps of this Exercise chapter, remember to continue practicing what you have learned here. At the risk of boring you with repetition, I will again list the core essential practices to promote lifelong weight management:

- Use your Log.

- Eat foods that provide carbohydrate, protein, and fat—and enjoy those foods in moderate quantities. Do not entirely cut out any favorite items; instead, enjoy them in controlled settings less often than you did when your weight was increasing.

- Try to always use the *Mouth/Hand Rule*, and most of the time eat at your *Designated Eating Place* while not reading, texting, watching, etc. (i.e., *No Simultaneous Activities*).

- Review and refresh the motivational material you have developed, and if you have not yet done that work, re-read *Chapter 4—Motivation* and do it.

- Pay attention to your self-talk to identify the *cognitive distortions* that knock you off course, develop *rational rebuttals* for them, and practice using them.

- Review your Log for high-risk situations and use the *CPR* tool to figure out how to more effectively navigate them next time they occur.

EXERCISE FOR PARENTS

As always, the most powerful lesson you can give your children is your own behavior. Increasing the level of Natural Activity in your daily patterns and possibly adding some structured exercise routines, will help your children learn that movement is a normal and enjoyable part of life.

You can further help your kids by reworking the family's idea of 'together time' if much of that time involves viewing shows or playing video games. There is ample evidence linking screen time with obesity. The more time people spend on the screen (watching shows, surfing the internet, playing video games), the more likely they are to be overweight and obese[32]. This applies both to children and adults so if you need incentive for finding interactive active family past-times, this is it.

Before I move off the subject of screen time, I am compelled to share with you additional information about children and screen time. Despite marketing campaigns touting the positive effects on intelligence of various baby- and toddler-training video products, the scientific evidence is simply not there. For children under the age of two, watching 'educational' videos does not result in any appreciable learning[33], and while older children may learn from screen sources, there is indeed significant harm in addition to obesity that comes of excessive screen time. Children and adolescents who have more than the recommended number of screen hours score more poorly on behavioral, social, and cognitive assessments[34, 35].

The American Academy of Pediatrics and the World Health Organization (WHO) recommend no screen time for babies under 24 months of age, except for video-visits (extremely important to grandparents!). Children between two and five years old should have no more than one hour per day of "high-quality" programs viewed together with their parents/caregivers. For older children, parents are encouraged to "place consistent limits on the time spent using media, and the types of media, and make sure media does not take the place of adequate sleep, physical activity and other behaviors essential to health." In other words, turn off the screen, make eye contact, and get moving!

If you are moving more, limiting screen time, and spending time with your children, chances are good that they are meeting the general recommendation of 60 minutes of physical activity each day.

CHAPTER 9

MISCELLANEOUS

Before we move ahead to the final chapter, Next Steps, there are a few hard-to-categorize questions that patients often bring up.

Can I sleep myself thin?

No. Unless you sleep enough hours of the day that you do not have time to eat (nor to work, study, love, and live), sleep does not make you lose weight. However, sleep might play a role in weight gain.

Poor sleep (consistently less than six or seven hours per night) has been linked to increased appetite (presumably because of associated hormone changes), reduced weight loss even when adherent to a healthy diet plan[36], and overall greater body weight and obesity[37]. The research in this area is still relatively sparse and I doubt any good scientist will tell you that your obesity is *caused* by insomnia. (Too bad, because we have some good insomnia treatments!) However, if you are one of the many people who skimp on sleep, you may want to reconsider. Even if adding a few hours of sleep to your life does not make the pounds fall off, you will surely feel more energetic and alert with a good night's sleep—and that can translate into more daytime activity and easier everything else, including weight management.

NOTE: If you struggle with severe insomnia, either look for a therapist who is skilled in CBT-I (Cognitive Behavior Therapy for Insomnia) or a self-help book that guides you through the process. If your insomnia is characterized by multiple awakenings, snoring, morning headaches, and/or sore throats, please talk to your physician about having a sleep study as you may have sleep apnea. Untreated, sleep apnea not only ruins your sleep, it also increases your risk for cardiac events that could do considerably more damage than make you sleepy.

What is bariatric surgery?

Bariatric surgery is surgery designed to promote weight loss. First performed in the 1950s and accompanied by many dangerous side effects, the procedures have been refined and are now a reasonably safe option for obese individuals who have been unable to lose weight with less invasive means.

While there are multiple surgical techniques commonly used, they can be boiled down into having one of three impacts: (1) limit the size of the stomach, thereby causing you to feel full with less food, (2) interfere with food absorption (called "malab-sorption") resulting in less of what you eat being converted into energy or stored as fat, or (3) both limit stomach size and interfere with absorption.

What can I expect with bariatric surgery?

It is difficult to pin down a specific percent of excess weight lost as each study generates somewhat different numbers. However, it is safe to say that most patients lose between 50% and 75% of their excess weight. (It is important to recognize that if you are extremely obese, losing even 75% of your excess weight will likely result in you becoming less obese or overweight, but not necessarily shift you into the healthy weight range.)

The weight loss that follows bariatric surgery is also often accompanied by improvements in obesity-related medical problems such as diabetes, hypertension (high blood pressure), hypercholesteremia, hypertriglyceridemia, sleep apnea, joint pain, and others. However, if the surgical patient fails to follow through with the necessary behavioral changes (pretty much everything I talk about in this book), the weight tends to return along with the medical problems.

Is bariatric surgery safe?

As with any surgery, there is the risk of death during or immediately following the procedure. However, if done by an experienced, competent surgeon, the risk is relatively low.

Once the risk of surgery and its immediate aftermath is over, there are ongoing risks and side-effects. A detailed discussion of the short- and long-term medical consequences of surgery is best left for a conversation with a bariatric physician. Suffice it to say that weight loss from surgery does not come without its price. While most who have undergone the procedure say the cost is worth the result, it is important for anyone considering the surgery to go in with her or his eyes open to the fact that the surgery is not a "fix" but rather a trade-off.

The "trade-off" of bariatric surgery is between the benefits of weight loss and the long-term challenges of having a smaller stomach and/or malabsorption. Weight loss with surgery requires the same trade-offs that weight loss without surgery requires— you trade off easy paths (e.g., eating whatever whenever, spending leisure time on your behind instead of your feet) for more demanding ones such as planning, scheduling, prioritizing, and moving.

Is bariatric surgery right for me?

Bariatric surgery is not a fix. Yes, it can make you feel more full on less food and yes it can prevent a portion of what you eat from being absorbed—but it cannot make you stop eating when you become full, nor can it prevent you from eating enough to compensate for malabsorption and consequently either not lose weight, or gain weight.

In the first year or two following surgery, most patients do pretty well in terms of compliance with dietary and exercise recommendations. They have jumped screening hurdles, spent considerable money, and endured major surgery and its aftermath—they are motivated! Motivation combined with the physical sensations resulting from surgery help patients stay on track. However, the motivating power of those physical sensations lessens as the individual gets used to them, plus the physical intensity subsides with time and healing. What this means is that the surgical patient has a limited length of time during which the surgery actively helps him or her to make the lifestyle changes needed to sustain long-term weight management.

Bariatric surgery is an incentive, a big stick, to change what you eat, how much you eat, when, where, and why you eat, as well as when, where, why, and how much you exercise. However, that stick gets smaller with time. If you are thinking that weight loss surgery sounds like just as much work as weight loss without surgery, you are right.

The answer to the question 'Is weight loss surgery right for me?' is, 'Maybe.' Clearly, it will not *make* you lose weight unless you put in the effort, as is the case without surgery. If you are facing imminent severe health complications consequent to obesity, and have not been able to reduce your weight with the reasonable approach outlined in this book, then perhaps a surgical kick in the pants is what you need. However, think carefully before you sign up. Investigate the surgeon you are considering and work closely with a psychologist to identify the strengths and weaknesses you bring to the undertaking. Do not go into this with the unrealistic belief that the surgeon holds the answer to your food and exercise difficulties.

How do I evaluate the 'proof' in product ads?

When making healthcare decisions, be cautious about whose advice you seek and on what products and programs you spend your hard-earned money.

The first red flag in product claims is reliance on testimonials. One or two or 100 people reporting satisfaction with a product does not mean it truly is effective, nor that it will necessarily work for you. What testimonials do tell you is that the marketer found some people willing to say they like the product—for free or for payment. Determining the effectiveness and safety of products or programs requires well-executed scientific studies—and even those claims must be looked at critically.

When marketers tell you about scientific studies that support their claims, there are a few questions that are critical to ask of the 'evidence' before you decide whether the product is truly effective and safe, or whether it is merely snake oil.

- **Are there multiple independent studies that support the effectiveness and safety of the product?** One positive study is a terrific start but definitely not enough to entrust with your safety. If the seller cannot point to several positive studies conducted by different groups who do not profit from the product, I would not trust it with my health.
- **Do the studies include a sufficient number of participants to conclude the results are not unique to the few people in the study?** When evaluating the effect of a product on something as complex as weight management, it is not enough to show it works on a handful of participants who may well have been hand-picked for that very purpose. If I am entrusting my body or my wallet to a product, I want assurance that it is safe and effective for a wide variety of people.
- **Do the studies include control groups along with the experimental group?** Control groups are those study participants who, instead of the product being evaluated, are given either a placebo (fake but believable treatment) or an established effective treatment the new product is hoping to equal or exceed. If the studies offered as proof of the product do not include reasonable control groups, they are basically worthless.
- **Are study participants randomly assigned to control versus experimental groups and are the people conducting the study blind to participants' group assignments?** In a nutshell, this means that neither the people administering the product/treatment nor the participants receiving it should know which group participants are in. Obviously, if the participant knows she or

he is receiving a placebo, it will not work. Conversely, if he or she knows it is the real product, the *expectation* of effect can create an effect whether or not the product actually works. Additionally, if the people administering the treatment and placebo know which they are administering, there are many ways, intentional and unintentional, they can skew the results.

- **Do the studies acknowledge their own weakness?** As we have discussed many times throughout this book, there is no 'perfect' possible in human endeavor. This applies equally to scientific method. Good studies conducted by ethical scientists will always include a discussion of the limitations of their work. This helps you be confident that the researchers are more interested in finding right answers than in proving they are right.

Will acupuncture help me lose weight?

There is a small set of studies that have evaluated the impact of acupuncture on weight loss. Some have found it to be helpful, while others have not. To my knowledge, we have yet to see published properly-designed studies that report meaningfully greater weight loss among patients undergoing acupuncture than those receiving placebo treatment.

Can hypnosis make me lose weight?

No. Hypnosis is not magic. It is a form of focused concentration that can help with relaxation and, while in the hypnotic state, enhance suggestibility. To my knowledge, however, there is no scientific evidence that it results in lasting change to your food and activity preferences, or your ability to cope with difficult emotions or circumstances. Ultimately, weight management comes down to actively taking the steps we have discussed throughout this book.

Why weight "management" instead of "control"?

If you were paying attention when you asked, "How do I control my weight?", you know the answer to this question. You cannot control your weight. I cannot control my weight. No one can control his or her weight. What we all *can* do, is *manage* it; and we do that by adopting the attitude (self-talk and beliefs) and the actions that tip our calories-in/calories-out balance in favor of a healthy weight range.

CHAPTER 10

NEXT STEPS

At this point, we have talked about realistic expectations regarding your shape, weight, and behavior change. My sincere hope is that you are fairly consistently, but not perfectly, doing the following:

- Reminding yourself why you picked up this book in the first place. In other words, tapping into the motivating thoughts and feelings that started you down this path.

- Tracking your behavior.

- Challenging your cognitive distortions.

- Enjoying a variety of foods in amounts that meet your nutritional needs, fill your belly, and do not stuff you.

- Opting to move under your own steam whenever possible, and incorporating more structured physical activities to build cardiovascular and muscle strength.

When you achieve your target weight range and fitness level, just keep doing what you have been doing. There is no 'maintenance phase' to begin. All the work you have done from the very first moment you began working this book has been maintenance. You have (imperfectly) maintained attention to your choices, intention to monitor and track your behavior, and reminded yourself that this is important to you. You have made some small and some large changes to your behavior and become aware of thought processes and habits that had been landmines and are now management targets. Each time you tripped and slipped, you learned something about what makes you tick and added that to your ability to take better care of yourself. All of that is progress and all of that is maintenance.

Obviously, your next steps are to keep doing what you have been doing—and remember there is no perfect, simply good enough.

Log forever! Really?!

Yes. To some degree, you will always benefit from self-monitoring. It does not matter whether that takes the form of the Log I have introduced in this book, a digital notepad or spreadsheet, or some other format. The important thing is that you do it.

As you move through life, it is inevitable that the format of your self-monitoring will evolve with your changing circumstances. That is good. It means you have actively incorporated the practice of self-awareness into your life.

How do I make my goals smart?

Smart goals are those that clearly define realistic objectives given your available resources. You can read about SMART goals all over the internet where they are usually defined as goals that are Specific, Measurable, Attainable, Realistic, and Timely or Time-bound. While these five attributes are definitely important, they need a little discussion if you are using them to set weight management goals.

Specific—Set specific goals about things that are within your control. For instance, recall that I said we cannot control our weight, only those actions that influence it. For example, in place of a goal of "lose X pounds," you are better off with a goal to "limit intake to XXX calories per day on most days of each week to promote weight loss."

Measurable—If you are targeting behaviors, as I hope you are, it is easy to count each time you, for instance, eat in your *Designated Eating Place* or hit your daily step target. Pounds are also countable but not within your control so if they are your focus, you may be setting yourself up for frustration.

Attainable—Despite encouragement to set behavioral rather than weight goals, I know there is a good chance you will still be interested in a weight goal. If so, please do not set large weight loss goals. If you are shooting to ultimately lose more than 20 pounds, set intermediate goals of five to 10 pounds. Twenty, or 70 or 135 or … can ultimately happen for you, but not soon enough to make you feel the progress as you step through the day-to-day challenges of behavior change. Setting your sight on a goal that is reasonably within reach, however, makes it exciting as you hit target after target.

In setting attainable behavioral goals, keep in mind that there is no perfect and striving for perfection will ultimately cause problems. As you assess your achievement of behavioral goals, remember that 'mostly' hitting them, and 'fairly consistently' are good enough, and that ***good enough is really good!***

Realistic—While some things may be theoretically attainable (e.g., participating in a triathlon within a few months), they may not be realistic (e.g., you only recently learned to ride a bike and have not yet learned to swim). As you set goals, take a step back and assess your skills and resources with the eye of an outside observer who does not know you very well. If that perspective suggests this is a realistic goal, go for it. Otherwise, scale it back—either in scope or timeline.

Timely or Time-bound—This one is tricky. If you are truly following my guidance and making gentle changes to your lifestyle, setting deadlines needs to be done very carefully. For instance, if the goal is to work up to a certain number of minutes of cardio exercise endurance by a specific date, and you do not hit that target, you risk feeling defeated and losing steam (remember the *What the Heck Effect*). On the other hand, if your goal is to engage in cardio exercise on no less than (a reasonable) percentage of the days in the month, the likelihood of hitting it is pretty good and the month target gives you a metric you can then track and use to adjust your strategy or goal accordingly.

The sample goal I provide under Specific above, "limit intake to XXX calories per day on most days of each week to promote weight loss" meets all SMART criteria. It specifically states XXX calories/day on most days of the week allowing you to count the number of days on which you accomplished it. It is attainable and realistic in that XXX is not an unreasonable target and 'most' days does not set you up for banging your head against the brick wall of perfection. Finally, it is time-bound in that it is tied to over 50% of days per week.

What questions should I ask myself?

There is an additional encyclopedia-sized book I could write for you in response to this question—but I will not do that today. Every person is unique and hence every situation that person faces takes on a unique flavor as a function of who is experiencing it. In other words, no one set of questions will be useful to everyone even in similar situations.

In place of that impossible encyclopedia, I offer you the three most frequently useful questions my patients have learned to ask themselves as they navigate the weight management path:

1. *How has having chosen to reject a temptation (e.g., a second helping or excessive quantity, skip a workout, etc.), negatively affected my quality of life?* In other words, has resisting an unhealthy temptation made your life worse? In almost all cases, the answer will be no, not at all. Answering this question will help you use this knowledge proactively to make healthy choices in future tempting situations as you remind yourself that you have 'survived' skipping that temptation in the past.

2. *What prediction about this situation am I making that is triggering me to feel the way I do right now, and what is the realistic probability of that prediction coming true?* Again, in most cases those catastrophic predictions are not at all likely to come to pass. Identifying these cognitive distortions lets you revise them to something more reasonable, less anxiety-provoking, and hence less powerful emotional overeating triggers.

3. *What made me want to actively manage my weight in the first place?* Answering this question on a regular basis will help keep your motivation fresh by maintaining your focus on what matters more to you than whatever momentary distraction is threatening to derail you. Periodically, pull out your *Pros/Cons Matrix* to reread and update the notes you made at the outset of this process about what was important to you.

Having done nothing, what do I do now?

Ask yourself whether this is as important to you as you thought when you started this book. If the answer is yes, ask yourself whether this is the right time. If you currently have so many competing demands for your attention, you may simply not have sufficient residual energy to undertake something as intense as changing long-standing behavior. First, however, there are a few considerations that deserve your attention.

If your life is one of constant overload, there are two paths you can follow. One is to figure out a way to carve out energetic space in which to attend to your health, building on the fact that you are already well-practiced at multi-tasking and juggling. The other path is to conclude that weight-management is never going to be part of your life so learn to embrace your body the way it is and enjoy the life you have.

If now *is* the time for you to get the upper hand on your weight-related behavior, here are the nitty-gritty, bare-bones, get-started steps.

1. Complete your Pros/Cons Matrix.
2. Start your Log.
3. Commit to a Designated Eating Place (DEP).
4. Use the Mouth/Hand Rule.
5. Engage in No Simultaneous Activities while eating.

When you have completed your *Pros/Cons Matrix* and have at least a month of the five nitty-gritty behaviors under your belt ('under your belt' meaning 'mostly', not perfectly!), go back to the beginning of the book and gently work your way through it again.

What if I haven't lost a single pound?

If you have been using most of the recommendations in this book most of the time for several months and you have not lost weight, and your physician has ruled out medical reasons for that, schedule a visit with a Registered Dietitian to figure out an eating plan to meet your unique biological needs and help you lose weight. If that option is not available to you, then it may be time to consider a Diet.

What's the best diet for me?

In deciding what structured diet to adopt, keep in mind that the only plan you will be able to stick with long enough for it have an impact must:

1. Be based on real food (not food-replacements) that provides fat, carbohydrate, and protein—all three macro-nutrients are essential to survival. Severely restricting, or worse attempting to eliminate, any one of them will put you at risk for both health and psychological problems.

2. Flexibly accommodate any special dietary needs you have due to medical conditions and/or allergies.

3. Include foods that you like. Forcing yourself to follow a menu that does not include your favorite items will leave you feeling deprived and make those items all the more enticing. Ultimately, this type of plan results in short-lived adherence followed by out-of-control overeating.

4. Honor your traditions. As we have discussed, sharing meals is an important component of our social relation-ships. If the plan does not allow you to enjoy your tradi-

tional food-related celebrations, you will quickly give it up.

5. Be designed to result in a gradual weight loss of one to two pounds per week over time. Tempting as it may be to adopt a plan that promises rapid loss, chances are slim that you will be able to keep at it for very long as it will undoubtedly be rigid and too low-calorie. Further, because of its impact on your metabolism, you will likely gain more weight than you lost when you inevitably quit.

6. Serve as a blueprint that you can adapt as your body changes and you shift from weight loss to weight management mode. If the plan is not one that can be followed the rest of your life with only minor adjustments, it will simply become one more diet with which you lost and then gained weight.

How long must I keep this up?

Only until you want to gain weight.

APPENDIX—SAMPLE LOG

Date/ Time	Food & Drink Consumed	Place/Doing	Context
MON. 12:30 PM	Salad w/sunflower seeds, dressing	Desk @ work	Busy day
5:30	Chicken/veggie frozen dinner	Kitchen	Tired, still hungry after eating
6:10	1 slice toast & butter	Kitchen	Still really hungry/tired, guilty
6:25	1 bowl Cheerios w/skim milk ½ c Rocky Road ice cream 3 cookies Grapes	Kitchen Living room w/ TV	Couldn't stop!!!
TUES. 12:20 PM	Salad (just greens), no dressing	Desk, working	Making up for last night's binge
2:30	Pkg cheese & crackers (6)	Desk, working	Not on my plan but I'm starving
5:30	2 scrambled eggs w/mushrooms, bell peppers, 1 oz cheese	Kitchen, reading	Light dinner after unplanned cheese/crackers
6:30	2 slices toast & butter Ice cream Grapes 1 Oreo, 4 Thin Mints	Living room w/TV	Restless, tired, feeling empty, meant to just have the toast since they could have been part of the eggs meal, lost control
WED. 8:00 AM	Yogurt/granola sundae	Desk @work	Gift from boss, couldn't refuse
12:30 PM	Turkey sandwich, iced tea	Deli café	Out with co-workers
3:20	Chocolate Kiss	Desk	"Prize" during staff training. Shouldn't have but it would have been weird to refuse
6:25	Angel hair pasta w/olive oil, salad	Kitchen	Daughter surprised me w/ dinner, couldn't say no. Surprisingly, it felt okay.

Date/Time	Food & Drink Consumed	Place/Doing	Context
THUR. 11:30 AM	4 Chocolate Kisses	Desk @ work	Starving. Mark shared leftover Kisses from yesterday's training, couldn't resist.
1:00 PM	Salad (no dressing, no cheese)	Desk, working	Guilty for big meal yesterday, knew I couldn't resist more if I ate in the cafeteria so brought salad to my desk.
5:45	Frozen dinner (chicken/veg)	Kitchen	Tired.
7:00	Tbsp almond butter Container fat-free yogurt 3 Oreos w/1 glass fat-free milk handful pistachios	Kitchen Living room TV	Oh s—t!
FRI. 8:30 AM	2-egg-white veggie omelet	Chez Wayne's	Breakfast meeting – crazy guilty for this after last night's binge but no way out of it.
1:00 PM	Turkey sandwich	Desk	Was going to skip but Mark offered to bring me a sandwich and it felt too weird to refuse since he knew I'd not had anything since breakfast. Also, I was hungry!
6:20	Low-fat frozen meal (beef something)	Kitchen	Boy that tasted good. Weird. Exhausting day.
SAT. 9:00 AM	Cheerios & milk, coffee	Kitchen	I love Saturday!
1:30 PM	Caesar salad	Restaurant	Lunch & shopping w/sister.
3:25	Mocha coffee drink	Starbucks	Little guilty about the calories but it was cold and yummy.
6:30	Frozen dinner (chicken/ veggie)	Kitchen	Going salsa dancing this evening!
SUN. 8:00 AM	1 bowl Cheerios w/2% milk 1 Toast & butter	Kitchen w/daughter	Maybe breakfast will help...
1:20	Salad w/sunflower seeds, dressing 1 c yogurt w/fruit	Kitchen	Am I eating too much?
4:30	String cheese, apple	Patio	
6:30	Chicken breast, 1 c broccoli, dinner roll w/butter ¼ cantaloupe	Kitchen Radio music	Forcing myself to do this ... freaking I'll gain weight.

ABOUT THE AUTHOR

Brenda L. Wolfe, Ph.D. is a Clinical Psychologist who has specialized in the study and treatment of obesity and eating disorders for more than 40 years, mastering the ability to translate scientific knowledge into practical guidance. As a result, she has helped countless people achieve their wellness goals. Now, semi-retired with time on her hands, Dr. Wolfe has authored the book she wished her patients had before they sacrificed years on the diet roller-coaster. *A Diet is the Last Thing You Need: Weight Loss & Maintenance Answers* organizes the best of weight science into easy-to-follow strategies that help you achieve lasting weight management.

In addition to clinical expertise, Dr. Wolfe brings to her work rich experience in both academic research and design of commercial weight loss programs. She has lectured to audiences across the United States, and published academic articles as well as self-help books, including *Get Your Loved One Sober: Alternatives to Nagging, Pleading, and Threatening* (with Robert J. Meyers) which received the Association for Behavioral and Cognitive Therapy **Self Help Book Seal of Merit Award.**

Dr. Wolfe makes her home in New Mexico where her life is rich with family, friends, and meaningful work. Her writing goal is to share the wisdom she has gained through her work to help readers enrich their own lives.

A REQUEST

Please take a moment to review this book on Amazon, or wherever on the internet you find your next reads. Your feedback will help me to improve it for future editions, as well as help others find it who might benefit.

Thank you

Brenda L. Wolfe, Ph.D.

REFERENCES

1 Marlatt GA, & Gordon JR (Eds.). (1985). *Relapse Prevention.* The Guilford Press.

2 National Heart, Lung, and Blood Institute. (1998). *Clinical Guidelines on the Identification, Evaluation, and Treatment of Overweight and Obesity in Adults: The Evidence Report.* (NIH Pub No 98-4083, 1998). National Institutes of Health. https://www.ncbi.nlm.nih.gov/books/NBK2003/

3 National Weight Control Registry. http://www.nwcr.ws/default.htm

4 Zomeño MD, Lassale C, Perez-Vega A, Perez-Fernández S, Basora J, Babió N, ... & Castaner O. (2021). Halo effect of a Mediterranean-lifestyle weight-loss intervention on untreated family members' weight and physical activity: A prospective study. *International Journal of Obesity,* 1-9.

5 Miller WR, & Rollnick S. (1991). *Motivational Interviewing: Preparing People to Change Addictive Behaviors.* The Guilford Press.

6 Schachter S. (1971). *Emotion, Obesity, & Crime.* Academic Press.

7 Schachter S, & Gross L. (1968). Manipulated time and eating behavior. *J. Personality & Social Psychology,* 10(2), 98–106.

8 Castellanos EH, Charboneau E, Dietrich MS, Park S, Bradley BP, Mogg K, Cowan RL. (2009). Obese adults have visual attention bias for food cue images: Evidence for altered reward system. *Int. J. Obesity*, 33(9): 1063–73.

9 Nijs IM, Muris P, Euser AS, Franken IHA. (2010). Differences in attention to food and food intake between overweight/obese and normal-weight females under conditions of hunger and satiety. *Appetite*, 54(2): 243–54.

10 Lorien EU, Weber JL, Heyman MB, Schichtl RL, Verstraete S, Lowery NS, Das SK, Schleicher MM, Rogers G, Economos C, Masters WA, & Roberts SB. (2016). Energy Contents of Frequently Ordered Restaurant Meals and Comparison with Human Energy Requirements and US Department of Agriculture Database Information: A Multisite Randomized Study. *J of the Academy of Nutrition and Dietetics*, 116(4): 590–598.

11 D'Anci KE, Watts KL, Kanarek RB, & Taylor HA. (2009). Low-carbohydrate weight-loss diets: Effects on cognition and mood. *Appetite*, 52(1): 96–103.

12 Power ML, & Schulkin J. (2009). *The Evolution of Obesity*. The Johns Hopkins University Press.

13 Contreras-Rodriguez O, Cano M, Vilar-Lopez R, Rio-Valle JS, Verdejo-Roman J, Navas JF, Martin-Perez C, Fernandez-Aranda F, Menchon JM, Soriano-Mas C, & Verdejo-Garcia A. (2019). Visceral adiposity and insular networks: Association with food craving. *Int'l J Obesity*, 43(3):503–511.

14 Ryan KK, Woods SC, & Seeley FJ. (2012). Central nervous system mechanisms linking the consumption of palatable high-fat diets to the defense of greater adiposity. *Cell Metabolism*, 15(2):134–49.

15 Jensen MD, Ryan DH, Apovian CM, Ard JD, Comuzzie AG, Donato KA, ... & Yanovski SZ. (2014). 2013 AHA/ACC/TOS guideline for the management of overweight and obesity in adults: A report of the American College of Cardiology/American Heart Association Task Force on Practice Guidelines and The Obesity Society. Journal of the American College of Cardiology, 63(25 Part B): 2985-3023.

16 Office of Disease Prevention and Health Promotion. (2015). *Dietary guidelines for Americans, 2015-2020.* US Government Printing Office.

17 Berkowitz RI, Moore RH, Faith MS, Stallings VA, Kral TV, & Stunkard AJ. (2010). Identification of an obese eating style in 4-year-old children born at high and low risk for obesity. *Obesity*, 18(3); 505–512.

18 Bohon C, Stice E, & Spoor S. (2009). Female emotional eaters show abnormalities in consummatory and anticipatory food reward: A functional magnetic resonance imaging study. *Int J Eat Disorders*, 42(3):210–21.

19 Bohon C, Stice E. (2012). Negative affect and neural response to palatable food intake in Bulimia Nervosa. *Appetite*, 58(3): 964–970.

20 Spitzer RL, Yanovski S, Wadden T, Wing R, Marcus MD, Stunkard A, Devlin M, Mitchell J, Hasin D, Horne RL. (1993). Binge eating disorder: Its further validation in a multisite study. *Int J Eat Disorders*, 13(12): 137–153.

21 Varnado PJ, Williamson DA, Bentz BG, Ryan DH, Rhodes SK, O'Neil PM, ... & Barker SE. (1997). Prevalence of binge eating disorder in obese adults seeking weight loss treatment. *Eating and Weight Disorders-Studies on Anorexia, Bulimia and Obesity*, 2(3): 117-123.

22 Snider SE, DeHart WB, Epstein LH, & Bickel WK. (2019). Does delay discounting predict maladaptive health and financial behaviors in smokers? *Healthy Psychology*, 38(1): 21–28.

23 Amlung M, Petker T, Jackson J, Balodis I, & MacKillop J. (2016). Steep discounting of delayed monetary and food rewards in obesity: A meta-analysis. *Psychological Medicine*, 46(11): 2423–2434.

24 Bradford WD. (2010). The association between individual time preferences and health maintenance habits. *Medical Decision Making*, 30(1): 99–112.

25 Barlow P, Reeves A, McKee M, Galea G, & Stuckler D. (2016). Unhealthy diets, obesity and time discounting: A systematic literature review and network analysis. *Obesity Review*, 17(9): 810–819.

26 US Department of Health and Human Services. (2018). President's council on sports, fitness & nutrition.

27 US Department of Health & Human Services. (2015). Surgeon General's Call to Action. https://www.hhs.gov/surgeon-general/reports-and-publications/physical-activity-nutrition/walking-executive-summary/index.html

28 Tremblay MS, Warburton DE, Janssen I, Paterson DH, Latimer AE, Rhodes RE, ... & Duggan M. (2011). New Canadian physical activity guidelines. *Applied Physiology, Nutrition, and Metabolism*, 36(1): 36-46.

29 UK Chief Medical Officers' Physical Activity Guidelines. (2019). https://assets.publishing.service.gov.uk/government/uploads/system/uploads/attachment_data/file/832868/uk-chief-medical-officers-physical-activity-guidelines.pdf

30 World Health Organization. (2004). Global strategy on diet, physical activity and health.

31 Sturm R, & Cohen DA. (2019). Peer reviewed: Free Time and Physical Activity Among Americans 15 Years or Older: Cross-Sectional Analysis of the American Time Use Survey. *Preventing Chronic Disease*, 16.

32 Stiglic N, & Viner RM. (2019). Effects of screentime on the health and well-being of children and adolescents: A systematic review of reviews. BMJ open, 9(1): e023191.

33 Anderson DR, & Pempek TA. (2005). Television and very young children. *American Behavioral Scientist*, 48(5): 505–522..

34 Walsh JJ, Barnes JD, Cameron JD, Goldfield GS, Chaput JP, Gunnell KE, ... & Tremblay MS. (2018). Associations between 24 hour movement behaviours and global cognition in US children: A cross-sectional observational study. *The Lancet Child & Adolescent Health*, 2(11): 783-791.

35 Madigan S, McArthur BA, Anhorn C, Eirich R, & Christakis DA. (2020). Associations between screen use and child language skills: A systematic review and meta-analysis. JAMA pediatrics, 174(7): 665–675.

36 Papandreou C, Bulló M, Díaz-López A, Martínez-González MA, Corella D, Castañer O, ... & Salas-Salvadó J. (2020). High sleep variability predicts a blunted weight loss response and short sleep duration a reduced decrease in waist circumference in the PREDIMED-Plus Trial. International Journal of Obesity, 44(2): 330-339.

37 Worthman CM. (2008). After dark: The evolutionary ecology of human sleep. In WR Trevathan, EO Smith, JJ McKenna (Eds). *Evolutionary Medicine and Health: New Perspectives* (pp 291–313). Oxford University Press.